# PROBLEMS OF PSYCHOTHERAPY

# PROBLEMS

# PSYCHOTHERAPY

*HERBERT ZUCKER*

**THE FREE PRESS,** *New York*

**COLLIER-MACMILLAN** LIMITED, *London*

Cop.5

# PREFACE

*T*HIS BOOK studies a number of issues which have continuously been at the center of psychotherapeutic work. It does not approach these issues in terms of a methodical review of the literature or through an examination of prevailing theoretical positions. Rather, it is a somewhat old-fashioned report of sustained and systematic experience in working with people and the bearing of such experience on psychological concepts, problems and procedures. It takes this form in affirmation of the view that continuous immersion in direct clinical experience is one of the major

v

means for testing psychological concepts and for developing fresh variations of psychological knowledge.

There is perhaps another warrant for a temporary release in every career from the "literature" and the strictures of authoritative knowledge. Psychology itself has demonstrated that in an ambiguous field close contact with the intensely-held opinions of others affects even the perception of physical objects. Personality is, in many respects, such a field, and thus there is every likelihood that absorption with authoritative findings and positions may well blunt by degrees one's own edge in perceiving reality. Actually, the book simply reflects the form in which I found myself working, probably for these very reasons. As an appreciative heir of academic psychology and psychoanalysis, I believe this form, though not in the current vogue of research, is rooted in productive naturalistic conceptions which have always been part of psychology.

I particularly wish to thank Drs. A. Ben-Avi, I. Chein, and N. Freydberg for their discerning and useful commentaries on various sections of the book. My wife, Bess, has been involved over the years with every aspect of the book, from ideas to punctuation.

HERBERT ZUCKER

# CONTENTS

# PROBLEMS OF PSYCHOTHERAPY

# *One*

# A VIEW OF THE FIELD

*THE WORD problems* is included in the title of this book advisedly. Alternative terms such as *principles* or *methods* are not quite satisfactory because they give no hint of the difficult and uncertain status of most issues in this field. Even the classic problems of psychotherapy, probed now for over seventy years and illuminated brilliantly in certain respects, nevertheless remain unsettled. What are the factors involved in psychological distress? What is the nature of change: which aspects of personality are alterable and to what degree? What are the most ef-

1

fective means for entering into another person's life? What can be done to improve the scope and depth of the therapist's use of himself? What conditions enable the person in therapy to meet himself authentically and in depth. What are the conditions of meaningful experience and effective communication? Is there an optimal balance of affect, sensation, and intellect, and how is it achieved? What constitutes useful therapeutic material? Given the uncommon social character of the therapeutic arrangement, what adjustment of artificiality and naturalness can be attained? What are we aiming for in therapy? These questions are not new, yet they can be asked again without being in the least superfluous.

### Expectations About Psychotherapy

Unaware of this state of affairs and other peculiarities of the subject, students enter the field expecting to be instructed in the theory and practice of therapy and then to be able to apply this instruction in subsequent practice. Naturally enough, they assume that available knowledge is roughly equal to the problems they will face in the field. They can hardly foresee that long-standing, basic questions remain unfathomed; that although we have some meaningful general answers, they cannot be applied with precision; that certain questions have to be answered afresh in each individual case. Nor can they anticipate that problems of personality and therapy cannot be grasped at proper depth through instruction but can be known only through firsthand, continuous experience of a certain sort. Psychotherapy is one of those fields one never really knows until one is well along in it, and even then one's grasp of it changes from period to period. Although psychotherapy legitimately professes to have a body of knowledge useful in dealing with problems of living, still as a profession it is unique in many respects. The conditions and expectations usually associated with professions such as engineering, law, medicine, or chemistry do not necessarily apply in psychotherapy.

Consider for example the character of work in this field. Work in the area of personality change ranges not from the easy to the difficult, but rather from the difficult to the impossible. There is no easy case and seldom does the therapist have the experience of being able to accomplish all that was hoped for. This circumstance is related to many conditions of the work, not the least of which is the problem of professional control of one's subject matter. The substance of psychotherapy (a person) is less subject to the control of the therapist than is the material of most other professions. A surgeon implanting a muscle, a chemist synthesizing hormones, is in control of his material to a degree unknown in psychotherapy. In contrast, the therapist depends on, welcomes, and works through the very forces that limit his control. Given this situation, what concept of professional responsibility fits this work? Responsibility for another person is assumed on the basis of the absence of essential powers in that person, in terms either of age, knowledge or competence. The assumption of responsibility by the professional rests on the possession of appropriate complementary powers. In medicine, for example, the concept of responsibility developed from experience with physical disease, in relation to which the patient has relatively little competence or control. What concept of responsibility is appropriate to a material—a person—characterized by self-possession, by the capacity for choice, having important if incomplete knowledge about the very problems for which he seeks help, who is the ultimate judge of what is useful and satisfying to him and who in most instances has a degree of competence and control not significantly different from most individuals in this society, therapists included? What are the implications for responsibility of a material that has a unique potential to be realized, that must at once be affected and yet not intruded upon? With regard to the expert himself, psychotherapy not only makes a call upon the therapist for knowledgeability, but upon his character, spirit, and personality as well. Few fields require so total and continuous a personal response as does psychotherapy. Given these conditions, other professions cannot readily be used as models for the psychotherapist.

## The More Likely Encounter

In the first stages of training, the aura of beginning attenuates the realization that this work is arduously uphill at best. Beginners, after all, are entitled to states of perplexity and discouragement without having to take a decisive measure of their field or themselves. Besides, our teachers and theorists have a great deal to offer. They show us many paths: as we work we come upon familiar landmarks, we affirm the utility of certain tools, we observe definite effects. Competence often appears to be in sight. Effectiveness with intermediate issues, however, is no guarantee of adequacy at other urgent reaches of this work.

Aptness in dream interpretation offers no assurance one will be able to help dissolve a barely noticeable chill wall separating a particular person from others. The literature abounds in material on dreams; very little is to be found on the latter problem. As experience stretches out, no sooner do we grasp one set of issues than another swirls up at us, making its own kind of call upon the personality and knowledge of the therapist. A sense of insufficiency is characteristic not only of beginners; it is a condition of this work from beginning to end, though hopefully it later becomes less pervasive.

Therapists react variously to the gradual disclosure of the nature of the field. Some persist in hoping someone has the answer, and this takes them on a round of allegiances to alternative theories. On this track the focus is more upon answers than problems. Other therapists hold on to what they have of promise and try to make it serve all necessities. Insight, for example, was buttressed by notions of levels, pacing, working-through, and so on, not wholly in an effort to refine the concept, but in part out of unwillingness to relinquish belief in its efficacy. Some therapists finally assent to the special shape of the subject and try to find the terms for a favorable association. For all its worth, prior knowledge is then taken as a preliminary guide for moving among problems that have few set answers. Indeed full appreciation of this knowledge requires that we put ourselves through the experiences that set the minds of our predecessors going. If we then take things for what they are, we will be able to stand on their work and perhaps also see something new on occasion. Freud quotes Charcot as saying: "He wondered how it happened that in the practice of medicine men could only see what they had already been taught to see. . . . he said that often he had to admit that he could now see many a thing which for thirty years in his wards he had ignored."[1]

## The Experiential Approach

These remarks remind us to cast a questioning eye upon what we are taught. In psychology and psychotherapy this teaching is a body of knowledge defining our understanding of people, of difficulties in living, and of means for resolving such difficulties. It is less the validity of this body of knowledge, however, than its methodological character that concerns us here. This book is based on the view that psychology as a subject matter has a number of unique features that ought to give direction to its theory and practice. This view especially emphasizes experience as the approach of choice in the field of psychology and psychotherapy. Unfortunately, the very familiarity of experience promotes a tendency to take it for granted. Yet it is so much at the heart of human psychology that it can hardly be passed over in this way.

As a concept, experience implies the unity of the person and of living and is, in effect, a definition of existence. Experience embraces the notion of the whole person; its units are molar rather than molecular or atomistic. It holds that the person takes shape under conditions of actuality, that is, by going through the events of living. In fact the term *actuality* is made up of almost equal components of activity and reality. Experience is based on the

1. Sigmund Freud, *Collected Papers*, I (London: Hogarth Press, 1946), p. 11.

tangible and the sensible rather than the descriptive and ideational, on direct participation rather than thought. Also implied is the claim to be a source of "truth," for the actual is practically synonymous with the factual or veritable. In sum, the concept asserts that to know life is to act in reality.

Experience refers to conditions of exterior stimulation as well as of interior response, to both the objective and subjective essence of living. Experience gives meaning to life and the meaning of life and at the same time creates a person who himself engenders meanings in others. Activity and reality play upon the entire person and out of this interaction emerges the whole range of human qualities. These qualities are addressed to the psychological senses—to perception, apprehension, contact, feeling, and so on. The gist or being of a person is not appreciable to the "surface" senses—to the eye or to the intellect. A person is expressed in terms of tones, compounds of flavors, which have more to be tasted and savored psychologically than to be inspected. A springy walk to the intellect is not the same as a springy walk perceived. The senses on which experience depends are fully activated under conditions of activity, reality, and wholeness. These last terms cover large areas of psychology and require considerable amplification. Such amplification as this book develops will come less through definition than through the representation of activities which incorporate these facets of experience and through the application of the experiential mode in the reconsideration of concepts and techniques.

The value of the experiential emphasis impressed itself upon me ever more concretely some ten years ago as it grew upon me that the special language of the dream is simply the language of experience. Entered into experientially the dream is a far simpler communication than many conceptions of dreams would have it. Just as dreams remain rather more unreliable and obscure to conceptual approaches, it may well be that other subjects such as schizophrenia, interviewing, and resistance remain enigmatic, not because of inherent complexity, but because of difficulties in experiencing these manifestations of humanness clearly. It is noteworthy that Sullivan, who cast a great deal of light on schizophrenia, summed up psychopathology with an experiential statement: "Everyone is much more simply human than otherwise."[2] The numerous implications of the experiential approach for many of the standard issues of psychology and psychotherapy should not occasion surprise, for these issues are not separate technical problems really, but rather only aspects of the entire person.

Experience is so much part of living that descriptions of this approach tend to elicit from psychologists and clinicians the remark: "But this is familiar. Anyway it is just what I do." Indeed it is impossible to function—either in living or as a psychologist—without employing the experiential mode. Yet, curiously, experience per se has not been a major subject of study in academic or clinical psychology, although recently there has been a surge of interest in this subject. Almost everything in academic or clinical psychology—motivation, perception, introspection, and so on—has a bearing on experience, but somehow the study of these separate topics never quite coalesces into a recognizable equivalent of full human experience. Ameri-

2. Harry Stack Sullivan, *The Interpersonal Theory of Psychiatry* (New York: W. W. Norton, 1953), p. 32.

can psychologists had, in fact, to search far afield, in Zen-Buddhism, for example, for conceptions of man centrally concerned with the nature of experience. The phenomenon of experience is yet to be explored by psychology in depth.

In any event we can hardly, in psychotherapy, afford an inadvertent or partial application of the methods of experience. In my opinion, clinical methods are currently a good deal more conceptual than experiential. There is a very real question about the degree to which psychologists deal with the shadows of experience rather than with experience itself. The shadows of experience are selectively meaningful to the intellect and are thus often mistaken for authentic experience. The oft-repeated response to descriptions of experiential activity, "Of course, this is what I do," is not borne out in fact. It is easy to identify with experience, but hard to generate it, particularly in artificial situations. With noteworthy frequency when clinical interviews are recounted in detail or studied on tape, it turns out that many clinicians are not implementing experience effectively. Even when this is acknowledged, a sustained effort is often needed to develop a working sense of the quality of experience and of approaches that promote it. It is a thread that may be all too readily lost, although for some persons functioning in this mode comes easily, if not naturally.

The familiar distinctions between intellectual and emotional experience, between facts and abstraction, are much too gross to cover the degrees and varieties of intellectuality so widespread in psychotherapy. Methodological antecedents and traditions have encouraged psychologists to become architects and arrangers of intellectual structures to a degree not fully appreciated. Refinement of conceptual structures is often prized above meaning or significance. In my view it is more difficult than many psychologists think to hold concepts loosely enough so that they do not intrude upon experience. This problem is not restricted to psychology alone. It can be seen in daily life and even in pure science. Bridgman believes that it was an unquestioning acceptance of classical physical concepts which left physicists unprepared for the upheaval wrought by the theory of relativity: "Reflection on the situation after the event shows that it should not have needed the new experimental facts which led to relativity to convince us of the inadequacy of our previous concepts. . . . a sufficiently shrewd analysis should have prepared us for . . . Einstein."[3] The problem is particularly crucial for psychology and psychotherapy because its subject matter is enormously demanding of the continuous experiential availability of both subject and student.

Obviously our activities in psychotherapy rest on the understanding that we have of human nature, but our understanding or knowledge is a function of the systematic aims and methods of psychology. In any field with a permanent frontier, where one aims to go and how one goes about getting there will determine what will be seen. Every psychologist, then, needs to inquire closely into the grounds upon which his work is based: What constitutes knowledge in this field? What kinds of knowledge are useful? What are the means for securing knowledge? By pursuing these questions we may come upon a number of methodological issues that have a bearing on the daily work of the clinician and perhaps on some aspects of general psychology as well.

3. Percy W. Bridgman, *The Logic of Modern Physics* (New York: The Macmillan Co., 1960), p. 1.

*Two*

# METHODOLOGY

*M*ETHODOLOGY in psychology has been greatly affected by the methods of the physical sciences, especially physics. In the realm of physical events the orderly control of intellect has produced imposing achievements, and this has naturally led to attempts to apply these methods to psychological phenomena. Psychology has benefited substantially from the general philosophy of method developed in physics, as has every other serious branch of knowledge. At its best, psychological training encourages an interest in the accurate description and understanding of reality, a respect for data, rigor in observation and reasoning, reflectiveness, a concern for verification, and a tendency to keep an open but discriminating and searching mind.

Psychology, however, has embraced not only the philosophy of the scientific method but in certain respects the very structure and content of the physical sciences as well. Some psychologists have maintained that the ultimate illumination of psychological phenomena will come only when these can be described in physicochemical or mechanical terms. Such concepts are regarded as somehow more basic and authentic than psychological concepts. (If this were the case we should expect physicists to be in a better position to advance psychology then psychologists.) However strongly this position and its variants are represented by certain psychologists, there are eminent physicists who are not inclined to agree. Heisenberg doubts that even biological phenomena can be satisfactorily explained on the basis of physical and chemical laws. "Concepts like life, organ, cell, function of an organ, perception," he writes, "have no counterpart in physics and chemistry."[1] Furthermore he believes that "The degree of complication in biology is so discouraging that one can at present not imagine any set of concepts in which the connections could be so sharply defined that a mathematical representation could become possible."[2] As for psychology, in his view "there can scarcely be any doubt but that the concepts of physics, chemistry and evolution together will not be sufficient to describe the facts."[3]

1. Werner Heisenberg, *Physics and Philosophy* (New York: Harper and Brothers, 1958), p. 102.
2. *Ibid.*, pp. 105–106.
3. *Ibid.*, p. 106.

Other aspects of the content of methodology in physics have been absorbed by psychology in like manner. Our purpose here, however, is not to trace this development; rather it is to point up that methods used effectively in one field are not necessarily applicable in another. Each subject matter requires a methodology appropriate to its own special nature. In this regard there are a number of aspects to psychology not quite duplicated in the physical sciences.

## Unique Features of Psychology

Psychology, to begin with, is the only field in which the subject studied and the student are one and the same phenomenon. When man studies the stars, atoms, trees, most animals, or neural structures, he is studying phenomena unlike him psychologically. These phenomena were undoubtedly totally incomprehensible to early man, for the absence of sameness is perhaps the first condition of ignorance. The more alien an object is from human psychology, the harder it is to understand at first. For this reason man's initial efforts to understand natural phenomena involved endowing them with human attributes. Animistic propositions assumed identicalness and in this sense represented a "legitimate" use of knowledge. Gradually it became clear that nothing could be known about trees, for example, merely because something was known about men. Identification with natural objects produced relatively few clues about their fundamental nature.

As man grasped that physical things are exterior to human psychology, he also perceived that so far as understanding and control are concerned, these things are connected to human beings largely in terms of perception and thought. It was a particular refinement of these human capacities that then advanced the understanding of physical objects. In relation to such objects knowledge is mediated by long processes of observation, by manipulation of these objects to bring out their properties, and by highly refined and rigorous modes of thought. Yet apart from rational comprehension of their properties, they remain alien to man. When a physicist tries to understand the atom, essentially he observes phenomena associated with it and thinks about it. He cannot apprehend its being because it does not exist in these terms; he cannot experience its nature except in a very limited way because it is nonpsychological in character. Its properties are selectively ascertained mainly through the application of higher thought processes.

When human nature studies human nature, the student and the studied share a potential identity that may be readily registered by both. This is possible largely because of man's consciousness, his capacity to be aware of himself and of objects around him. One of the special characteristics of his consciousness is that it registers psychological processes far more sensitively and comprehensively than it does physical processes. An uninstructed person knows less about his physical apparatus—the physiology of digestion, for example—than he does about his psychology. Members of a primitive society may not even be aware of the function of the brain, but it would be no surprise if they knew a good deal about the nature of fear and even of dreams. In studying human nature, then, psychologists study a phenomenon that is already a repository of data and knowledge about itself. The same holds true for the psychologist, who, even before formal study, is no less such a repository. The study of psychology never begins in ignorance; some individuals learn a great deal about psychology just in the course of ordinary living. A talented person may thus come to a substantial understanding of most of the vital concepts in psychology without direct recourse to this formal knowledge. Such a development would be very unlikely in relation to any of the physical sciences. In any case, given identity, such stores of knowledge are often interchangeable. The psychologist's study of himself is a form of studying other individuals; conversely, his study of others is a form of studying himself. In therapeutic work the therapist learns as much about himself through the opportunity to know other persons well as he ever learned through his personal analysis.

## Observation in Psychology

Man's variable but considerable sensitivity to psychological processes within himself is fundamental to the growth of psychological knowledge. The apprehension of processes and meanings, however, is not a function of observation in the conventional sense. Observation has the connotation of looking at, taking notice, attending to an object exterior to oneself. Yet this is not how psychological meaning and knowledge develop in typical living. A person generally goes through whatever he is doing—taking care of the baby, driving, talking to a friend—with no deliberate attempt to observe. Too much consciousness of self alters, if anything, the very events one wishes to observe. This is so even for simple actions: a person marking closely how he coordinates walking is likely to stumble. Even without any attempt to observe, however, varieties of meanings and understandings are spontaneously registered. Indeed unless some effort is made to keep meanings out of consciousness, one simply finds them in mind as an after-effect of experience, rising from a broad, organismic base. One may, for example, go through a pleasant, ordinary conversation and only minutes afterwards realize that one has gotten to know that this person is deeply dispirited. Psychological knowledge is thus more direct and less mediated than knowledge about physical objects.

From this point of view psychology is a naturalistic discipline, concerned with people as they are or have it within their nature to be, based fundamentally on empiric-experiential methods. Such a view has definite implications for methodology. If he is to understand human nature, the psychologist has first to go to great lengths not to disrupt the typical flow of psychological processes. Human nature radically transformed is not human nature. Artificial situations and basic alteration of physical processes (matter), so characteristic of the physical sciences, are inapplicable in the study of people. Heisenberg's statement of Bohr's view of the alteration of matter in the field of biology surely applies to psychology with equal force: "We are concerned with manifestations of possibilities in that nature to which we belong," rather than with experiments that change the nature of the subject.[4] Psychology has been cognizant of the need to carry out its studies in lifelike settings, yet much remains to be done to bring under study the range and depth of daily living. This problem is par-

4. Heisenberg, p. 155.

16

ticularly acute for the clinician, who sees people in the restricted situation of his consulting room. Yet conditions of study will always be limited in one way or another. The question is what can be devised, despite such limitations, to improve the opportunity for encountering the actualities of human functioning. Some of the possibilities for achieving this aim in the inevitably artificial clinical situation will be discussed in the subsequent clinical chapters.

If the necessity for naturalistic study is conceded, then the next methodological step is not observation as it is in the physical sciences. At this juncture the psychologist has to take his lead from the way psychological knowledge is developed in the course of ordinary living. People get to know things about themselves and others by going through events; psychological data and meanings are by-products of the general functioning of human faculties and systems. Prior to observation, then, the psychologist has first to make things happen to himself: he needs to be involved on the level of organismic experience; he cannot be on the outside observing, applying knowledge or thinking. The clinician, therefore, needs to arrange occurrences; he has to attempt to have happen in therapy what happened to the subject in life. Such an arrangement provides at least two major sources of information. By combining and identifying with the subject in the context of "events," the therapist may learn what such events bring out in the person. Also by going through these events, the therapist is seeing through the medium of himself how such events *tend* to affect a person. In this vein observation (if one wishes to call it such) refers to the crystallization of what has worked upon and in both the subject and the psychologist. Observation of this kind is a matter of determining what the self discloses in response to actualities; it is a process of activity and realization.

Certain developments in the field of psychology are altogether consistent with this methodology. It cannot be a matter of chance that the concepts that have illuminated human behavior most have come from working clinicians— Freud, Jung, Adler, Horney, Fromm, Sullivan, for example. This has happened, I believe, because the clinical relationship provides such a favorable opportunity for combining and identifying with people. Wundt and Freud, two men of comparable capacity, working in the same time period in similar cultures, evolved rather different conceptions of people mainly because they employed methods that differed in the use made of mind and heart. Furthermore, even the testing of major concepts has been carried on extensively in the framework of clinical methods. The testing of concepts by means of clinical procedures is slow and laborious and surely needs many refinements. Still, it has been mainly through the application of concepts in the clinical interaction that they have been found crucially wanting. This kind of direct trial, over time and experience, led to revision of libido theory; to redefinitions of the concept of anxiety; to changes in interpersonal theory; to the expansion of need systems; to the diminished use of personality types; to the virtual evaporation of the nosologies; and so forth. Despite these contributions, clinicians have always been made to feel a little ashamed of their apparent lack of scientific sophistication and rigor (the absence of laboratories, instruments, clear-cut experimental situations, and so on). General psychology might have done better had it not lighted so eagerly on some of the untidy aspects of clinical work; it should rather have tried to see what is involved in procedures that help generate such contributions.

## *Certain Methodological Aims Accented*

These considerations indicate that the largest methodological issue in the process of psychological study has to do with the use made of the human capacities and characteristics of the investigator. Instrumentation has failed because no apparatus has been devised that can combine with psychological processes and crystallize meanings through the medium of its reactions. No machine or apparatus, other than the human being, can register the peculiar character— that is, the sensory-experiential meanings—of psychological processes. Apparatus in psychology turns out to be chiefly a particular way of sampling behavior. Such samples may be more or less representative, but in the end the understanding they afford depends on the degree to which the psychologist is able to identify with the material developed.

Systematization of observation and thought has not been fruitful because the rules of organization have not been adequately related to the nature of the subject matter. This is not to minimize the value of the higher thought processes; obviously they are indispensable to the development of concepts and theories in psychology. Rather, the problem is to determine how they can best be used in the course of psychological study. Analysis, inference, and induction cannot precede adequate contact with the basic data, and such contact is perhaps the most difficult part of the process. Varying degrees of contact make for very different descriptions of "reality," so that what is deeply moving to one psychologist may be only sentimentality to another. Improving the observer's contact and attunement may help reduce the unreliability of observation. Such improvement can occur, however, only as we are able to answer certain methodological questions: What are the conditions of adequate contact with psychological subject matter? What is the nature of organismic experience (the source of psychological knowledge)? What arrangements enhance the chances of bringing such experience into play? In what ways can the observer's reading of his own senses be refined?

The problem of building a coherent body of knowledge, then, starts at the lowest rung of the ladder—that is, with the difficulty of establishing facts upon which psychologists can agree. From these varying basic descriptions spring the large assortment of theories and explanations available in psychology today. Psychology may even be said to be the study of the differences among psychologists in their views of man. Yet this situation is not unique to modern psychology. In every age diverse conceptions of man have, because of dissimilar elementary "facts," competed side by side over long periods of time without resolution. Two thousand years ago Cicero related disorders of mind and soul to such factors as greed and lust.[5] This prescient attempt to connect psychological difficulties to personal characteristics was engulfed over the ensuing centuries by such causal notions as the devil, disease, and heredity. Even

5. Gregory Zilboorg and George W. Henry, *A History of Medical Psychology* (New York: W. W. Norton, 1941), p. 65.

today some variant of the concept of disease hangs on as an explanatory idea in psychology.

Given an abundance of ideas and yet a tangle of disagreement, psychologists could well set the goal of clarification as a major methodological aim in the field. There is presently perhaps less need for concepts never before envisioned than for an approach to psychological actualities that will legitimately reduce elementary disagreements and ambiguity. Refinement of the operations of the observer promises to contribute significantly toward the implementation of the goal of clarification.

Another relevant methodological aim for psychology would be to find means to know in depth what there is to be known. Indeed it would be a methodological advance even to define the meaning of psychological knowledge held in depth. This is a crucial problem for psychology, because the utility of knowledge in relation to people and living seems peculiarly dependent on the level at which it is held. The absence of deep or growing individual knowledge makes alterations in personal direction seem prohibitively risky for professional as well as lay persons. Ideas, furthermore, may fall away not because of inherent deficiencies but because, unplumbed, the ideas do not manifest their true impact and value.

Possession of ideas, or even a grasp of ideas, is to be distinguished from profound attentiveness to their fate in one's own mind and experience. For example, the notion that a special use of time and resources are necessary for ideas to germinate can be "understood," restated, and even elaborated on by any intelligent person. Knowledge of this order, however, differs from Poincare's fine appreciation, based on years of personal experimentation, that the solution of mathematical problems depends on a delicate alternation of conscious and unconscious work and that the solutions are often a function of the perception of aesthetic harmonies.[6] His was a knowledge that affected his entire mode of working.

Often the contribution of important theorists in psychology is to reaffirm or deepen concepts already available in some measure. With Freud having moved parent-child interaction, at least structurally, to the center of the developmental stage, Jung observed with ground-breaking penetration the unconscious effects upon the child of subtle parental tensions and problems. Adler then noted that the child's special vulnerability is produced by his condition of relative powerlessness. Fromm and Sullivan examined the same issue and found love, tenderness, and justified faith an antidote to the "archaic terror appropriate to each person's history as a fragile and dependent infant."[7] (As this last quotation from a paper by Rochlin suggests the very character of a statement may indicate the level at which a concept is grasped.) It is mainly in terms of degree of emphasis and depth of reach in relation to an issue that the writers can be distinguished—which is not to underemphasize the significance of these differences of degree. The forward movement, then, of a concept in this field may in part be defined in terms of depth of affirmation or in terms of extension of depth or breadth, rather than mainly in terms of newness.

6. Henri Poincare, "Mathematical Creation," in *The Creative Process,* ed. B. Ghiselin (Berkeley: University of California Press, 1954), pp. 22–31.

7. Isaiah Rochlin, "Psychologist's Role in the Protection of the Public," an address reprinted in *Professional Digest,* New York Society of Clinical Psychologists, I, No. 4, (April, 1966), p. 5.

*The Search for Generality*

Psychologists have absorbed from the physical sciences other methodological aims that have questionable pertinence to their field. Dazzled by the widespread order achieved in the physical disciplines, psychologists adopted as their prime goal the discovery of the general laws of their field. Though this goal has been pursued with great energy and devotion, the yield has been negligible. One would be hard put to find any kind of law in psychology, let alone one that has the order and invariability of the law of conservation of energy. This does not mean psychology is barren; it may mean that this goal is unproductive.

The search for generality has taken various forms in psychological theory. One approach follows an assumption, serviceable in the physical sciences, that the highest form of invariability is to be found in laws or principles that reduce diverse phenomena to fundamental underlying unities. Thus in psychology theoretical systems have been developed in which certain factors or principles have been described as both general and central to human functioning. The factors considered to be central, however, have varied from system to system. In the clinical field, for example, each major investigator has seen a different factor at the core of personality development. In rapid succession we have been offered the following central propositions, each laying claim to greater centrality than its predecessor: the instincts, the birth trauma, the struggle against weakness and inferiority, disharmony between the conscious and the unconscious, lack of parental affection, lack of self-esteem, interpersonal insecurity. No doubt these propositions are recognizable as the work of Freud, Rank, Adler, Jung, and Sullivan. Every one of these concepts strikes a responsive chord because each describes some significant aspect of humanness. Each worker has presented an aspect of man that for complex reasons he is best qualified to describe. Each of these theories has a compelling application to some individuals and even a limited application to almost all individuals. Yet when one tries to understand the whole of an individual on the basis of one or another of these fundamental concepts, one is left with a great sense of insufficiency.

The remarkable number of propositions claiming basal significance may simply suggest there are a large number of factors involved in human functioning and that all of them are important. It is chiefly the disposition to follow the pattern of the physical sciences that is forcing assumptions as to what is primary or at the source. In this endeavor generality has often been confused with significance. A claim made in regard to significance somehow seems to infuse a concept with an aura of generality. Accumulated experience, however, has necessitated a gradual acknowledgment of the multidimensional character of personality. The history of psychoanalysis discloses an effort to correct the narrow emphasis on one or two or three central factors. We move from the neuroses to the character disorders, from interpersonal relations to ego-psychology and existential considerations, and so on. Each of these developments reflects the need to introduce additional working concepts so as to include all of the dimensions vital to an understanding of personality.

The effort to define what is fundamental is compromised

not only by the large number of factors indispensable to personality, but also by the ramifying, interdependent character of these dimensions—that is, by the complex unity of personality. In a specific person under particular circumstances seemingly remote factors may have a bearing on present difficulties. Jung, for one, believes that conditions such as failure to reach ideas developing in the mind, may in some people give rise to elaborate symptomatology. "I have often seen cases," he writes, "where abnormal sexual fantasies disappeared suddenly and completely in the moment when the mind becomes aware of a new thought or content."[8]

Reductionism places psychology in the position of trying, in effect, to determine whether bone is more basic than muscle. The ramifying, multidimensional character of personality renders dubious the search for and use of central factors or principles. Yet this is the basis on which so many clinicians proceed.

Even when not burdened by faith in reductionism, the pursuit of generality has had very hard going in psychology. The effective use of general principles requires that the conditions of application be consistent and uniform. In the physical sciences and particularly in the laboratory the number of forces affecting an event can be strictly controlled and thus the event can be consistently described by a principle. According to Philipp Frank, general concepts require "smooth" or "closed" conditions: "If we say, for example, that the law of inertia or the law of conservation of energy is confirmed by science, we mean only that there are in nature frequently conditions which can be regarded

8. Carl Jung, *Contributions to Analytical Psychology* (New York: Harcourt Brace and World, 1928), p. 152.

as smooth and can be, therefore, described by these laws. We must always have in mind that the facts of human behavior which are tested by psychology and sociology can hardly be described as smooth conditions."[9]

The human situation, in contrast, is a remarkably unsmooth or open system. At any one time, the human being is a function of complex interior physical and psychological forces, as well as forces emanating from a complex physical and social environment, all in a constant state of flux. The attempt to apply principles to this shifting welter of forces has given many a psychologist second and dim thoughts about his field. Although most psychotherapists have accepted the "unsmooth" terms of human experience as their universe of discourse, many have done so with the expectation that these terms and concepts would have the same systematic character as physical concepts, that is, a similar precision and generality.

Certain properties of human nature—such as consciousness, thought, feeling, uniqueness, emergence, will—deserve special mention for the mischief they play with the objective of finding general laws. Man can look at himself, consider his nature, appreciate the meaning of his existence, and direct his energies toward affecting himself or the world about him. Imagine the state of affairs in physics were an electron able to decide it didn't like the atom with which it was associated and begin to look for greener fields. Or suppose it became intrigued with the problem of being able to leap two instead of one millimicrons and then set itself an ingenious and arduous program for developing

9. Philipp Frank, "Psychoanalysis and Logical Positivism," in *Psychoanalysis, Scientific Method and Philosophy*, ed. S. Hook (New York: New York University Press, 1959), p. 310.

this facility. The physicist trying to build a laboratory around this sort of chap would before long acquire the wild-eyed look so familiar on the faces of psychologists.

A close look at the characteristics of some of our working concepts uncovers further obstacles to the possibility of generalization. We have in psychology a number of useful ideas, such as the unconscious, the libido, the power drive, the need for security, the ego. These are essentially descriptive concepts, derived directly from observation of people. They are organizing ideas that describe a particular dimension or process of personality in more or less general terms. Although they have many functional qualities, the interrelationships among these concepts cannot be stated in the precise terms that distinguish physical laws. Nor are they theories of the type found in physics; that is, they are not formulated as analogies to observed phenomena. In the sense that they describe observable phenomena these ideas are rather more like cell theory in biology than, for example, the quantum theory of light in physics. Although concepts in psychology are essentially descriptive, still they are often inherently explanatory. The mere notion of inferiority, or passivity, or the unconscious renders rational many phenomena in human behavior.

These concepts are examples of the general knowledge we have in psychology, but the kind of generality they possess needs to be further clarified. Findings in other fields have led psychologists to expect that the structural and functional aspects of a particular factor would tend to have comparable degrees of generality. In biology, for example, the eye has certain general structural attributes and these are consistently associated with certain general functional attributes. On the psychological level, whereas sex, unconscious processes, fear, ego functions, and so on are common to every person, the variability with which each of these dimensions operates in different individuals defies attempts to set down precise laws of functioning. Once able to identify fairly general structural dimensions of personality, psychologists slipped into assuming or hoping for equivalent functional generality.

It is plainly this variability of operation that renders the task of formulating lawful concepts so difficult. At the same time it is this very variability that is the source of individuality. The human being is as much unique as he is general. As a result of individual differences the operation of a dimension has precise order only in the unique terms in which it occurs in a particular individual (and even within the individual this order may change with a change of conditions). What he holds in common with others makes him recognizable as a human being, yet the individuality of the person imprints its stamp on the general (just as the general in the person is also present within his individuality). His identity, moreover, is defined not by the dimensions he shares with others, but by the differences that make up his uniqueness.

Our concepts, then, lack generality, the more so as we move from the physical, mechanical components of personality into the more purely psychological. This does not mean these concepts have no standing as knowledge. On the contrary, they are useful in our work both in terms of understanding and application. We have to concede that our concepts are open-ended; however, given the factor of uniqueness, they have to be to permit the final statement of order to emerge as an individual equation. General ideas in psychology usually have to be refined empirically for fit and the approach to refinement has to be made through individuality. Thus the absence of precise generality is not incompatible with order and application. The study of people is no more amenable to mass methods or mass application than is child rearing.

## *Meaningfulness*

In this field, therefore, the test of the value of a concept may not be generality per se, but rather meaningfulness. Concepts are meaningful when they deepen understanding and alert us to yet other important aspects of personality that in particular persons may be of special significance. Knowledge of such concepts facilitates application in that they permit work to proceed on the basis of recognition rather than the more arduous course of discovery.

If meaningfulness is taken as a measure of the value of a concept, it helps define further the qualities of useful concepts. In psychology meaning is affected by the degree of abstraction, so that concepts need to strike a balance between the concrete and the abstract. When there is too large a gap between a concept and its concrete manifestations, the concept becomes difficult to relate to life. Psychological behavior takes place in the here and now and is registered in specific ways. Some time ago an investigator discarded the word *mother* in favor of the term *caretaker*. This may have improved the level of operational clarity, but at the same time it evaporated the entire psychology contained in the word *mother*, the very area of experience he was seeking to study. Psychological phenomena can only be described in psychological terms. Love, as love, for example, exists only in the realm of experience. Many physical processes support this feeling, but they illuminate nothing of its psychological essence. There is nothing in physicochemical concepts through which one can approach a description of its experiential character. Psychological concepts require a certain degree of concreteness because they must have meaning for people. It is only within persons that the phenomena of psychology exist. And for individuals psychology exists in terms of the meanings of experience, which is in itself a particular universe of discourse, not translatable into other terms.

## Clinical Implications

Many of these methodological considerations have a direct bearing on clinical practice. These implications will be developed in the subsequent clinical chapters; however, there are a few points that may be stated here.

General conceptions do not place one in the position of knowing in advance what will be the significant issues in working with a particular person. Therapy can founder on the fact that a person has learned to generate just enough static so that although he sees and hears all, nothing really gets through to him. Unlearning such a character trait may be just as crucial to the ultimate outcome as anything the person comes across in the exploration of his family life. Preconceptions held too tightly narrow the possibility of responding to relevant considerations. Meanings in living and in therapy may vary rapidly. In a matter of minutes a person may move from irrelevance to contact, from genuine suffering to using this as a minor manipulative device. In therapy even as we pause at one connection, other relevant considerations come into view. One moves, as it were, in a shifting field, in which every motion is circular, every factor is connected to another, even as it spirals and circles. In therapy the significance of a factor is to be discovered in an individual only at a particular point in time. He may of course be in that state many times.

Beyond this, the peculiarities of psychological knowledge are such that the therapist really does not know the meaning of some of these concepts until he has met the factors to which they refer in experience. Transference in the textbook is only a pale representation of transference in therapy. Concepts in psychology are just bare bones; to be meaningful they have to be fleshed-in, particularly at the moment of application. They need to be qualified by the general character of the individual and, simultaneously, by interconnection with numerous dimensions of personality. By doing so, concepts become amenable to highly individual applications. It takes a long time to become a clinician largely because of the special way learning takes place in this field. One is prepared for psychotherapeutic work through extended study of meaningful concepts; in actuality, however, for a long time the clinician is trying out these concepts rather than simply applying them. At least this is what he should be doing if he ever expects to make such knowledge his own. Those who fail to do this are susceptible to distortions of the good sense in some of these concepts. The clinician, for example, who has grasped intellectually the concept of interpersonal insecurity but has not really felt it out for himself, may very well oppress the people with whom he works with an abundance of contrived acceptance.

Unless related to a substantial grasp of human psychology, technique is just a well-meaning shot in the dark. Indeed, techniques often mask large areas of ignorance. The use of the couch is a case in point. The hope was and is that a physical arrangement that reduces distraction would enable the person to reach profounder, otherwise inaccessible, levels of himself. Over the years the evidence for this has grown less and less compelling. Experience has shown that the capacity to face unpleasant or frightening aspects of self is much more related to certain psychological conditions (degree of personal competence) than to any physical arrangement.

In summary, psychology has to find its own methodological destiny, one based directly on the nature of its own subject matter. Upon this hinges the development and uses of psychological knowledge—methods of study, the character of understanding, and the conditions of generalization, abstraction, prediction, and application. The clinician can be no less involved with this area than any other psychologist.

# *Three*

# CLINICAL INTERVIEWING

*THE INCEPTION* of therapy has been formally designated as the Initial Interview. So much has been written about the issues of the first interview that it has acquired the status of a special phase of therapy. There are clinicians, however, who feel that the general objectives and methods of clinical interviewing apply as readily to the first as to any other interview.

Typically the first interview has carried the burden of defining the person's problems, establishing rapport, making a diagnosis, weighing the motivation for therapy, as-

33

sessing the person's therapeutic possibilities, structuring or defining the process of therapy, and so on. The therapist enters the initial interview with so many specific objectives and questions that he may easily lose sight of the fact that they cannot be pursued directly but are more or less resolved on getting to know the person. Sullivan draws attention to this effect when he observes that "the psychiatric interview is primarily designed to discover *obscure* difficulties in living which the patient does not clearly understand. . . . Such difficulties stand out more clearly and more meaningfully as one grasps what sort of person he is and what that person does and why."[1]

If this is what needs to be done then the special standing of the initial interview is diminished. It takes its place merely as the first of many that aim for the same goal. The concern in the first interview is not a particular catalogue of issues but rather, as in any other interview, to get to know the person.

## The Therapeutic Relationship

Of the issues traditionally associated with the first phase of therapy, one, the problem of rapport, has in fact a direct bearing on the possibility of getting to know the person. Rapport, the clinician is forever advised, is greatly facilitated by the presence of warmth, respect, and acceptance in the therapist. This is indisputable; yet such characteristics are not to be produced on demand. The quality of

1. Harry Stack Sullivan, *The Psychiatric Interview* (New York: W. W. Norton, 1954), p. 15.

rapport is largely a function of what kind of person one is, and is only trivially related to intention or technique. All urgings notwithstanding, the initial rapport will be simply what it characteristically tends to be for a particular therapist on meeting a stranger. If a therapist tends to be quiet, perhaps even reserved, in receiving another person, his simply being so lends at least that degree of substance and reality to the interview. A contrived response only gives rise to the inevitable unease or hollowness that attends an artificial situation. In a certain sense the less said about these desirable but difficult-to-achieve qualities the better, for heavy emphasis generates pressure to adopt roles. The clinician need only be reminded that his work requires a reasonable decency in his attitudes toward others and that lacking this he is already late in doing something about it.

For all that, respect for others is very variously implemented in actual living. By definition, respect for others is incompatible with attitudes of omnipotence, superiority, righteousness, or condemnation. Yet there are other forms of disrespect that emerge when respect and acceptance become a fetish. All-encompassing acceptance may be a variety of saintliness, which in its own way places the therapist above the person and more significantly, impairs his effectiveness. Attitudes such as "whatever you are or do is all right with me" may get in the way of understanding what the person is about. If the person is a master of the subtle barb, the therapist will not know what living with him is really like until he receives one, undefended by attitudes of cosmic benevolence. Acceptance precludes rejection or a totally unsympathetic response, but it need not involve approbation, consent, or agreement. Indeed if one's valuation (respect) is not to be delusive it has to include an appreciation of the person's limitations and deficiencies. When respect takes the form of a glowing faith in man's worth and potential, it often eventuates in underestimating what the person is up against and what still needs to be learned about growth and change. People are often lost or trapped, and despite their best efforts and those of the therapist a way out is hard to find. The view that the communication of acceptance and respect will comprehensively disentangle a person's potential amounts to assuming that every individual, under proper conditions of respect, will find the solution to problems that over the ages have remained obscure to the most profound students of human nature.

The qualities that enhance rapport need not be adopted ideologically or as articles of faith. Assuming a basic decency in the therapist, then the character of his acceptance of others, his optimism about human potential, will grow out of his experience. Perhaps the minimum condition underlying rapport reduces itself to being human enough not to be alienated by some of the unpleasant manifestations of humanness.

Beginners in therapy naturally tend to be somewhat more anxious and insecure in their first sessions. These preliminary tremors are not of much consequence; in the course of turning to the work the genuine qualities of the therapist's personality will emerge soon enough. Besides, it is always impressive how very human people are to therapists. Anxiousness, a piece of foolishness, or a real limitation of personality are very often taken in stride by them. Those people who make a habit of focusing on the inevitable frailties of the therapist define in the process some of their own characteristics, thus contributing to the day's work.

The general quality of the therapeutic relationship, it should be remembered, is, in its essence, a professional relationship. People do not come to therapy to find fathers or friends, even if they start out that way. Ultimately they are concerned with straightening out their lives, not with getting the therapist to fill it. They may find it pleasant and even momentarily comforting that the therapist is friendly, warm, or lighthearted. In the end, however, they will value more his interest, seriousness, relevance, accuracy, skillfulness, and knowledgeability. These qualities will have a material bearing on the kind of relationship that develops. Although they may not swiftly place the relationship on a first-name basis, they do not preclude the flow of profound feelings toward one another. They do, however, leaven the interchange so that such feelings do not confuse or impair the relationship.

## The Process of Interviewing

In opening the first session it seems altogether natural to begin with what difficulties have brought the person, though other ways of beginning are not unknown. For some therapists it is a matter of some sort of principle to say nothing and see how the person opens the session—certainly never to ask what he is coming about. Such distortions of common sense in the name of technique have yet to be justified.

The person's first words about his difficulties are usually classified as his "complaints." This rather invidious designation coincides with a tendency to take these statements rather perfunctorily. The attitude seems to be that this is the usual formal beginning of therapy and such statements are to be heard out, but then we are to pass on to the real work of therapy (whatever that might be). This attitude may be partly an outgrowth of experience in the early days of therapy when people came with circumscribed symptoms such as, "I don't have much feeling in my left hand." For good reason the effort to extract psychological meaning from such statements turned out to be fruitless. Nowadays people usually begin with more meaningful statements about themselves, but these often are not opened up in a sustained way. Frequently the flow of the interview is diffused by the multiple objectives of the initial interview and by lack of clarity about how to reach into the first statements. Initial interviews often touch down lightly on a number of bases: the "complaints," getting identifying social data, answering assorted questions (What do you think is going to happen in therapy?), getting bits and pieces of mental status or some history, and so on. These first statements, however, should develop into some meaningful illumination of character, or else the participants have to understand how it is that they do not.

This brings us to the main work of the first and any other interview, which is to learn: Who is this person? What goes on in him? What is he made up of? A person may be regarded as coextensive with the way he lives. Ideally, the best way to know a person is to be with him in his daily life over a period of time and to be able to ask him at crucial moments what is going on in him. Although this is implemented in some restricted ways in therapy, such an approach is on the whole impractical. This leaves us with a difficult problem, for in the consulting room we have a limited range of events and therefore a relatively narrow sampling of direct behavior. Within this restricted range, however, the person relates to the therapist in much the same way that he does to other persons, thus providing the participants with a direct source of knowledge. Another advantage of this setting is that the person tries to make available his private thoughts and feelings, opening a realm not readily accessible even in the direct observation of behavior.

Still we have the problem of how best to tap the largest source of data about the person—outside experience. Transference notwithstanding, there is more to be seen of the person in the events of his daily life because these have greater range, intensity, and significance than the events of therapy and therefore call forth many more of his characteristics. By the time the person appears for the therapeutic hour, however, we have in him only residuals of these experiences.

This being the case, the task of the therapist is to help the person convert these residuals into an approximate form of the actual experience. There are many difficulties in such an endeavor. At best, experience is registered incompletely, with only degrees of awareness; also there are often unconscious efforts on the part of the person to suppress aspects of experience. To maintain states of unawareness and avoid pain, the person frequently develops characterological modes of reaction and expression that obscure unpleasant realities. Furthermore we have in therapy only words and expressive gestures with which to evoke daily experience, and these can be used just as readily to screen experience as to call it up. Nevertheless we can approximate actual experience to a greater or lesser degree, depending on how we go about it.

The extent to which we share in the person's life may be gauged by the character of the material developed in therapy. The more the material has the character of everyday experience, the greater the degree of sharing. Experience has the quality of actuality, of now, of acting and being acted upon, of living through events and being affected organismically through sensations, perceptions, feelings, and thoughts, with behavior and thoughts the resultants of this broad process. The therapeutic material, then, should re-create actual situations and persons; it should be sufficiently full-bodied to be infused with the organismic qualities of the person.

## Renewing Experience

It is a long step, however, from a general appreciation of these points to a refined and working sense of the gradations of actuality and fullness in a person's verbalizations. People do not readily duplicate the actualities of their lives in their talks with the therapist. More often than not they offer impressions, ideas, views, abstractions, and condensations. Such statements are not simple perceptual accounts; rather they are constructions derived from the events. As such they are steps removed from the events per se. Although such reports are not grossly intellectual, they are essentially so because they formulate rather than duplicate life. Because they are not entirely devoid of "meaning," it is easy to be snared into a response to them. Yet under the circumstances the point of contact will be an idea, not the person in events. Ideas about events are peculiarly vulnerable to being cast in terms that obscure the objective characteristics of the person. Outside of the detail and check of actualities, one idea or version may be as good as another. Intelligence serves to make the idea or version only more impregnable. A therapeutic exchange based on such material involves a give and take of notions, sometimes spirited, but at arms length from what is really happening in the person's life.

Overestimation of the utility of ideas as therapeutic material grows out of some venerable psychoanalytic concepts. Freud believed that symptoms were related to painful memories and ideas that had been forgotten or kept out of consciousness. This led to a particular conception of the unconscious—namely, that the contents of the unconscious exist most truly in the form of ideas or memories. Freud could never quite relinquish this view, even when he had to deal with the question of whether impulses and feelings can be unconscious. For the most part, he maintained, only the ideational representations of these processes can be considered unconscious.[2] Although he was not altogether satisfied with his attempt to distinguish between unconscious ideas and affects, he nevertheless summed up with the statement that "repression is essentially a process affecting ideas."[3]

These concepts conditioned therapists to accept ideas as the basic material of therapy. Troublesome ideas or memories rather than life experiences then become the focus of therapy. If one accepts these assumptions, then free association becomes the approach of choice, because it is

2. Freud, *Collected Papers*, IV, pp. 104–112.
3. *Ibid.*, p. 112.

much more likely to cast up ideas than would accounts of daily experience. A streaming of consciousness may very well bring up the recollection of once having wanted to strike one's father, for though long out of mind it exists as a memory. Take a person, however, who characteristically becomes combative when faced with a difficult problem. Unless this has been brought to his attention or somehow formulated by him, he will not be able to come upon this trait by means of scanning ideas or memories because it does not exist in this form. Many aspects of character are not available in the shape of ideas but can be seen only in social behavior.

To lay the basis for a mutual experience in therapy, the person has to bring in his life, not just to talk about it, but rather to narrate it authentically. Such an account calls for particulars concerning where, when, and what. Events need to be re-created in such a way that it is almost possible to visualize the scene and hear the actors. Statements have to build up images and not simply relay coherence or intelligence. If the person says that he has had a fight with his wife, then the conversation has to be heard word for word. Such duplication places the person back in the experience and brings into play the qualities that such experiences call out in him. The immediacy of the material then has the effect of catalyzing the therapist's participation.

The following is a clinical example of how summaries or impressions tend to remove the person from contact:

I went to my friend's home. It was quite an evening. We had dinner. And talked quite a bit. After a while I realized I wasn't really involved. Of course, I joined the conversation a number of times. But I knew I was really detached, thinking about other things. And this is the way it often is.

Actually this material was developed at much greater length, but the quote is representative of what was offered. This statement could easily be followed up with such questions as: Are you this way in other situations? When did you first notice this sort of thing? What other things were you thinking about? An analysis of the person's statements, however, reveals its dearth of content, making it questionable that it can be taken as a meaningful communication. "We talked quite a bit," but no mention is made of any subject. There is a reference to "we," but no indication of who was there. "I joined the conversation a number of times," but no indication of what she said. We have then her view that she receded and began to think about other things, which leads to her conclusion that she is detached. In all of this the therapist is dealing only with the person's conceptions. The larger event has not been reconstructed, thus the therapist lacks the material to develop his own sense of the situation. It is even possible that the person's summary does not reflect what actually happened. If we could have heard the conversation, we might have found that it was about politics, that the person was relatively uninformed on these matters, that she made one or two feeble sallies to take part in the discussion, which left her feeling vulnerable, and that she then drifted off into thoughts of what an unaesthetic turn the conversation had taken. In short, contact with the actual conversation might have revealed that detachment describes this experience very inadequately.

The following excerpt, set down immediately after a clinical interview, illustrates both the difficulty of and necessity for developing material that has the quality of actuality.

This person is a 20-year-old male dropped for academic failure after his first year of college. Personally he is able but very restless and has considerable difficulty in getting things done. At this point, the fifth hour in therapy, he is about to apply to another school for part-time study. He is in the process of trying to select three or four courses for the coming semester.

P: I am thinking of registering tomorrow. How I say I am thinking! I am going to register tomorrow. Barry my cousin is also going to school. He's going with a girl whose father feels he ought to have an education—if the father is going to feel all right about Barry going with his daughter.

T: What courses are you considering taking?

P: Well there are lots of courses I can take. But I got all jumbled up by my mother getting into the deal. I don't know. Maybe I ought to live outside the house. She promised me she wouldn't nag or get into things but she can't keep her promise. Before I knew it she was going over the bulletin, suggesting things she thought I might like.

And oh yes!—They feel I should take courses only for credit and not just audit them. They say I won't feel its a challenge unless I take it for credit.

(*Here we have his view that his mother is to blame for the difficulty he is having in selecting some courses. In passing he proposes a solution. As yet, however, we have very little material on what actually occurred, merely his summary of the experience.*)

T: When did you talk to them about this?

P: Let's see. Was it Saturday or Friday? Not Saturday somehow. I think it was Friday. After I left here on Friday I went down to the college, got the bulletin, found out what I'd have to do to get in, and then I went home.

After I got home, I told my parents that I thought I'd like to go to school instead of working. That I was thinking of sitting in on a couple of courses. They said then that it ought to be a real program and for credit or they wouldn't support it.

T:    When did you try to select some courses?

(*The therapist's questions are directed simply toward what happened. A question such as the one above tends to bring things down to earth, out of the realm of summaries, opinions, and abstractions.*)

P:    Let's see. Was that on Saturday? No I didn't do that on Friday or Saturday. It was Sunday. After Curly called. Asked me to go to a party. No it couldn't be Sunday. There aren't parties on Sunday. Let's see. It was Sunday. (*This interview took place on Tuesday following the weekend to which he refers.*) In fact he called me at about two. Then from two to three I went up and looked over the bulletin. Then I got tired of it and played my guitar for a while. Then my mother came up, asked what I had done, lay down on the bed, and began to look through the bulletin. I hadn't stopped, though, I was just taking a break.

T:    How did your mother happen to come into it?

P:    Well she always says I'll never do things unless I'm pushed to it.

T:    Was the guitar a signal in any way that you were in trouble?

P:    Well I had only stopped for a while, I hadn't given it up.

(*The therapist's conjecture is premature. The event it-*

45

*self is still so undeveloped that the person does not yet have a basis for considering this possibility.*)

T: Suppose you try to say what went on before she came up?

P: Well I worked on it from two to three. First of all I think the bulletin is poorly organized. It's hard to know anything in it. On one sheet they list all the courses, just list, that you can take for credit. No descriptions.

T: Couldn't you refer to the bulletin for the description?

P: Yes, but it was confusing. Then my brother came in. Just talked and talked—about what's going on with the basketball team. I wondered whether he was trying to subvert the efforts I was making. Soon he left but by this time I was very nervous so I picked up my guitar.

T: How far had you gotten before he came in?

P: Oh, I checked off a lot of courses. There was one on Atheism and Skepticism that looked interesting. Another on Existentialism. Another on the Economics of Socialism. I'd like to take the Introduction to Economics, because its given by an outstanding instructor, but I already have two courses in Eco. There was also a course on Jazz. One on Poetry. I wondered if I could substitute Jazz for a music appreciation course. I'd like to take courses that would help get me standing as a sophomore. I checked off about 15 courses I could take.

After my mother came in I didn't get anywhere with it. She lay down on the bed and began to read off course descriptions to me. (*A brief pause.*)

Oh by the way last night when I went to bed I felt dizzy and saw some images. Is that a matter of medical concern? (*This occurrence was discussed briefly. It turned out that he had gone to bed fatigued, having had that day some tranquilizers as well as antibiotics for an*

*infection. The person appreciated the necessity for visit-*
*ing his physician should the dizziness reappear. It was*
*never again reported as a symptom subsequently.*)

 *T*: Did you work on selecting courses further—after
your mother left?

 P: Well, on Monday. After I went to the doctor. I
went into a cafe, looked at the catalogue, but I didn't
have a pencil and couldn't get anything done on it. And
today I handed out leaflets on the Birmingham affair.

 T: Were you able to select among the 15 courses you
had checked off?

 P: No. When I listed the courses I couldn't find them
in the main bulletin. When I found one in the bulletin I
couldn't find whether it was given for credit. I had to
keep looking back and forth between the courses listed
for credit and then see what it was about in the bulletin.
It was too confusing. I got very nervous, tense when I
was working. (*More to this effect.*)

 T: It was too much for you—sort of overwhelming.

 P: I felt it all over me in all my muscles—just the
way I feel now talking about it.

 T: Then it comes down to the fact that it is very hard
for you to make this kind of choice—which you haven't
quite acknowledged is the main thing about this episode?
Isn't that so?

 P: Yes.

 T: But then we have to see what goes on in such a
situation that throws you.

By developing the actualities of the event, he is able to
crystallize some of the real issues affecting him. For most
of the session the person is nowhere close to the sense that
the difficulty in selecting courses is peculiarly and substantially his own. By recreating the episode, he finds himself

literally experiencing the difficulty and unable to diffuse it by references to his mother, brother, disorganized bulletins, or alarming images. Although this is not a complex or profound apprehension, it is not an inconsiderable achievement in therapy for a person to take an aspect of himself for what it really is. The energy generated by this kind of experience is an important source of change and tends gradually to improve the person's sensitivity, objectivity, and relevance in future movements.

## Other Qualities of Useful Material

In addition to actuality there are certain other essential properties of material useful in therapy. The material has to be fresh as opposed to being stored, prepared, or stale. Freshness is not necessarily a function of the age of the material; it is not limited to recency. Rather it has to do with the person's mode of functioning, with whether there is a new vivification in each response. In this vein there is really no such thing as the same old stimulus calling out the same old response. The material has also to be sufficiently intense to evoke at least the minimum feeling tones necessary for fusion with experience; mechanical, dry, contained language is devoid of warmth and leaves the persons uncombined with what is being described. Material has to be relatively intact, as opposed to scattered, vague, or rambling, because the latter by definition, are out of touch. Finally, it has to be reasonably basic and simple to be one and the same with experience; material that is consistently complex and abstract is by its very nature removed from actuality.

This is not to say that therapy cannot be undertaken unless the material is endowed with all of these features. Few people come into therapy with these properties unimpaired. They are pointed up because they are vital to the task of making experience common to both parties, which is the foundation of all further work. Moreover, deficiencies in these qualities can be worked with directly. They do not necessarily improve by themselves with the uncovering of personal psychodynamics. In fact insight may be vitiated if it is developed without laying the ground for effective communication. A person who talks coherently but with a deep almost imperceptible tonelessness about incidents has long ago hit upon a mode for neutralizing experience. Trying to take a history from such a person or trying to establish the actualities of an event is like asking someone to sing who has forgotten the sound of music. The presence or absence of these qualities in the person's material usually defines certain important issues about the person's general integration. These incapacities then become the first order of business, not psychodynamics or breadth of coverage. Clearly, for these issues to get the attention they warrant the therapist has to have some working knowledge of the "chemistry" of experience.

## The Issue of Commitment to Therapy

Commitment, an issue often associated with the first interview, refers to the general question of what a person really means to do about himself. It is a strong word, preferred by many clinicians to the term motivation, because it connotes a quality of pledge or determination in relation to self deemed to be essential to the difficult work of psychotherapy. As an issue, it is by no means restricted to the first interview or even the early stages of therapy. The peculiar nature of therapy makes what the person really means to do about himself a decisive concern in every phase of therapy. Unlike so many aspects of medicine, therapy is not a procedure in which something is done to the person. In therapy the significant discoveries and experiments have finally to be made by the person himself. Therapy attempts to lay the ground for these ultimate activities, which may be undertaken only as the person comes into possession of himself. At this point, when at least a minimum degree of self-understanding and integration has been achieved, the person's readiness to sustain a struggle with the issues of his life probably becomes the crucial factor affecting movement and growth. All of the procedures of therapy are affected by the person's motivation, from the simple elaboration of incidents to final achievements. Not that therapy requires perfect motivation; the concern need only be that motivation not fall below a certain minimum required to get anything at all done. As varieties of motivation are encountered in relation to different kinds of problems, a basis is gradually developed for making a judgment as to what constitutes such a minimum. When motivation falls below this point, no matter how much talk is going on, the work is at a standstill. Under these circumstances some special, and perhaps drastic, kind of intervention on the part of the therapist may be necessary.

The therapist needs to be alert to the ebb and flow of this factor. Some therapists try in the first session to take a reading on this matter. Thus the person may be asked what he thinks is going to go on in therapy—in the expectation that something of his motivation may be reflected in his conception of therapy. The person, for example, who believes that there will be a sudden resolving revelation may spend less time working than waiting for the millennium. As with so many other plausible devices, however, there is in practice a meager yield to this question. The response is usually limited to a more or less conventional statement of what the person has heard about therapy. The more information people acquire about therapy the less useful such questions become. In any event misconceptions held in innocence or ignorance do not matter very much because they yield to experience. Conceptions vehemently maintained more often than not are positions selected because they rationalize unacceptable needs so well.

Direct or ingenious questions rarely succeed in tapping the character of commitment. Rather a sense of this factor grows out of the presence or absence of certain qualities in the general material. In this connection it is of particular importance to note whether the material reflects a quality of search. For example, a person reports in characteristic fashion the following incident:

> I went out bicycle riding with the family. Before we got started my son walked his bike through the water and my husband shouted at him. I just shriveled up when he did that. And then the younger boy fell off his bike. After that I was very nervous and kept my eye on him—I didn't enjoy a thing. Of course, my husband didn't do a thing about it. And sure enough he fell off again.

Though it may have taken perhaps fifteen minutes for the incident to be recounted, the condensation communicates the essential overtones. These appear to be: "My husband is harsh, irritable, and uncaring. His ways agitate our family life and leave me bruised, on edge, dismayed." The incident draws attention to her husband's "difficult" characteristics, whereas it represents her as sensitive, put upon. Nowhere in this portrayal is there any effort to find something about herself. Reports typically lacking in this dimension indicate a very slender thread of commitment.

In addition to search, there are other bases for measuring the quality of commitment. What effort is made to bring in troubling experiences and to consider disagreeable possibilities about oneself? When encountered, are such experiences and issues carried—that is, do they work in the person or do they noiselessly drop out of sight? Does the work of therapy remain verbal or does it in palpable ways reach into actual living and behavior?

The factor of commitment affects the answers to these questions, but by no means exclusively. As other considerations are taken into account it becomes clear that the concept of commitment is not unitary or independent but rather shades into related factors, which explains the somewhat blurred character of the concept. This renders it difficult to make a simple application of the concept. For one thing, every working clinician appreciates that however distinct may be the desire for change, inevitably it is counterbalanced by forces opposed to change. In concrete situations, it is often hard to determine whether one is dealing with weak motivation or strong resistance. The problem may not be so much that the wish to change is faint but that it is nonexistent, so to speak. In a particular person, a certain orientation, such as the wish to be the favorite, may be so deeply embedded that his truest desire is to achieve this aim and the possibility of altering it is never genuinely entertained. In short, the determinants of a weak disposition for change varies from person to person so that the analysis of commitment may spiral off into complex patterns.

The concept of commitment has to some extent (along with associated ideas such as "drive toward health") occupied the position of a sacred cow in psychotherapy. This is not to minimize the bearing commitment may have on outcome; however, these overarching concepts have a way of intimidating therapists, so that they do not look beyond them. Behind the sweep of these "ultimate" postulates lie concrete considerations that the clinician needs to identify and work with. The capacity to mean to do something about oneself involves congeries of psychological factors (potency, hope, seriousness, spirit, and so on) that in themselves may be therapeutic issues. The presence or absence of a quality of commitment may be decisive in terms of outcome, yet its relative absence does not require that therapy not be undertaken or that it be discontinued.

## Structuring

Structuring refers to any description of the process of therapy or any instructions regarding procedure offered by the therapist, usually in the early stages of the work. Such orientation or direction is assumed to help the person get underway. Much of what is usually offered, however, is either superfluous or not particularly meaningful to the person.

In a typical example of structuring the therapist may say at some appropriate point: "We're here, of course, to talk about your problems and difficulties. Your job will be to talk about yourself and particularly about situations in which you have some sort of difficulty. We will go through this material and try to understand what makes for the difficulties you are having." Superficially, this is a perfectly rational statement that renders the process dimly conceivable and thus may reassure both person and therapist. It vaguely represents what the therapist would like to have happen, much of which the person is unable to grasp because the statement is deceptively simple. The third sentence in the statement, for example, refers to so complex a process that it could not possibly have much meaning to the person.

If the therapist has sufficient clarity about what needs to be done and goes about doing it, structuring for the most part turns out to be redundant. As for the first sentence of the hypothetical structuring statement, in all likelihood the session will already have begun on the question of what difficulties bring the person to consult with the therapist. The suggestion that the person must participate in the development of material will have been implicit in the therapist's activity long before it would have been useful to state it. Built into the way the therapist responds or asks questions are directions defining effective collaboration between person and therapist. Appropriate participation on the part of the therapist discourages yes or no answers, rambling, or superficiality; underlines the importance of the person's initiative, of genuine communication and understanding; and helps to develop a meaningful reconstruction of life experiences—without the therapist having to pause to lecture about any of these issues. In short, the sense of therapy and its procedures should in general derive from activity and experience rather than from instruction.

## The Therapist's Preliminary Description of the Issues

At some point in the first or second session it is useful, as Sullivan suggests, for the therapist to offer a statement specifying how he sees the person and the issues of the work thus far. The following is an example of such activity:

> You strike me as a person who can describe himself very perceptively; you even account for a good deal about yourself, but you seem to live as if you don't really know what you know. However much you know, it doesn't come into your life as a basis for action. At bottom you seem uncertain, confused, and unable to take a step. Though you seem a considered person, I suspect that when you do move, you do so impulsively. You seem to end up not really going by your inclinations, whether positive or negative, but instead just closing your eyes and leaping into space, hoping for the best.

The more such impressions are documented and amplified by concrete examples taken from the material of the hour, the more effective the statement. There are, of course, occasions when the material is barren or the person is very hard to get to know. This in itself, however, is descriptive. Such an interview may make it evident that the person is highly contained, rather removed from himself, and only grudgingly acknowledges inner experience. Although these observations define a negation of personality structure, they are no less characterizing than any other description of personality. In most cases then some useful summary statement can be developed.

Such statements tend to have several effects. To begin with, they afford the person an opportunity to consider issues about himself judged to be significant by the "expert" with whom he has consulted. This in its own right is one of the essential experiences of psychotherapy. As a result, the person gets a chance to learn what is going to go on in this work. Having met the reality of this process to some degree, he is then in a better position to weigh whether this is what he really wants to do. At the same time, with the therapist having placed his preliminary professional judgment on the table, the person can form some opinion about the relevance and capability of the therapist. (Difficult as it may be, the person carries the responsibility for evaluating the service he is receiving—as is the case in every significant venture he undertakes.) Conversely, the person's reaction to the summary may give the therapist some notion of how the person will take to this work, and it may bring into the open issues on which the entire future of the venture may hinge. Although such a summary may not be possible in every case, the tendency to make one increases as experience enables the therapist to formulate such statements with greater ease.

## An Interview Examined

A widely discussed first session reported by Gill, Newman, and Redlich[4] provides an excellent opportunity for

4. Merton Gill, Richard Newman, and Frederick C. Redlich, *The Initial Interview in Psychiatric Practice* (New York: International Universities Press, 1954), pp. 132–205. I wish to thank International

a concrete analysis of the issues of the initial interview and of certain problems of interviewing. The person interviewed is a thirty-year-old married woman who called the clinic on her own for an appointment. The interview is conducted by an experienced psychiatrist. A number of the exchanges between the person and therapist are excerpted below. The discussion paralleling the interview material consists of my comments on the therapeutic interaction. For another view, see the running commentary on the same interview in Gill, Newman, and Redlich.

Universities Press and the authors for permission to use the excerpts presented here.

INTERVIEW

т.*1:* Will you sit there. (*Softly.*)

p.*1:* (*Sits down.*)

т.*2:* (*Closes doors.*) What brings you here? (*Sits down.*)

p.*2:* (*Sighs.*) Everything's wrong I guess. Irritable, tense, depressed. (*Sighs.*) Jus' . . . just everything and everybody gets on my nerves.

т.*3:* Nyeah.

p.*3:* I don't feel like talking right now.

т.*4:* You don't? (*Short pause.*) Do you sometimes?

p.*4:* That's the trouble. I get too wound up. If I get started I'm all right.

т.*5:* Nyeah? Well perhaps you will.

p.*5:* May I smoke?

т.*6:* Sure. (*Pushes ashtray toward patient.*) What do you do?

p.*6:* (*Sighs; takes cigarettes out of pocketbook and lights one.*) I'm a nurse, but my husband won't let me work.

т.*7:* How old are you?

p.*7:* Thirty-one this December. (*Exhales smoke forcefully.*)

т.*8:* What do you mean "he won't let you work?" (*Clears throat.*)

p.*8:* Well (*Clears throat*) for instance I . . . ah . . . I'm supposed to do some relief duty two weeks (*Sighs*) this month . . . next month, September, and he makes it so miserable for me that I'm in a constant stew. (*Sighs.*) And he says that my place is home with the children. I

### DISCUSSION

T.2: This opening is appropriate, to the point, down-to-earth.

T.3: Probably this comment was intended to encourage further expression on the part of the person, but it amounts to meeting vagueness with ambiguousness. If our objective is to get into actualities, the person has to learn that this is what has to be done and also has to be helped to do it. A response in this direction would have been: "What sort of thing gets on your nerves?"

P.2–5: The person begins in vagueness, feels as if things are being done to her and tends to blame others for her difficulties (P.2). Taken in conjunction with her reluctance to talk about herself, we have early signs of a distinct resistance.

P.6: In this remark the person returns to a charged area of her life.

T.7: For some reason the therapist needs time to absorb this remark, because he responds irrelevantly in T.7 by asking for her age, but comes back in T.8 to the point.

T./P.8–10: In answer to T.8 the person indicates she and her husband apparently fight about her taking on even temporary work in her field. There is also some difference between them about her role in the home. Finally she hints she feels hemmed in and restless with

INTERVIEW

agree, but I wa . . . I need a rest. I need to get away from them. I can't stay closeted up in the house all the time.

T.*9:*   How many kids are there?

P.*9:*   Two.

T.*10:*   How old are they? (*Clears throat.*)

P.*10:*   Three . . . five months.

## Discussion

the children. In P.*8* the person defensively merges several
important themes in a manner that probably makes it
difficult to single out any one of them. The therapist tries
to find some footing by asking for some facts (T.*9, 10.*)
Although these facts are not irrelevant, note that his request for self-limiting facts does not result in the eluci-
dation of any of the themes of P.*8.* Indeed by P.*12* the
person is involved largely in an account of her husband's
problems.

Whatever else may account for the somewhat inefficient
responses of the therapist, one factor is that the therapist
is not clear about what he is trying to do. In some diffuse
way he is trying to get to know the person, but he seems
unsure of what this means and of how it is done. Each
time he stands on the threshold of a situation to be absorbed and understood, he is deflected into establishing
certain facts, such as the person's age, number of children, husband's occupation, (T.*7, 9, 10, 13, 15, 16, 17,*
and so on). It may be that he takes this tack on the basis
of an old assumption of diagnostic interviewing that such
facts are prerequisites to understanding the person. As the
transcript shows, this kind of question and information
affects so little, has so little energizing value, that it takes
the person nowhere. Time and again, it is the person
rather than the therapist who returns to hint at a charged
issue (P.*6, 11, 14, 16,* and so on), although there are a
number of occasions when the therapist helps to keep a
meaningful current flowing (T.*2, 8, 12,* and so on).

Understanding this woman calls for the re-creation of
scenes from her life, so that the qualities such events
bring out in her are reanimated and thus become available to be experienced. If one were to move in this direction, P.*8* would draw some such question as: "I gather

INTERVIEW

T.*11:* Mmmhnn.

P.*11:* (*Sighs.*) Oh it isn't only that. It's a million things.

T.*12:* Tell me some of them.

P.*12:* (*Sighs.*) Well to begin with, there are a lot of things I didn't know about him before we got married that I should have known—at least I feel I should have.

T.*13:* You've been married about four or five years?
P.*13:* Four years . . .
T.*14:* Mmm.
P.*14:* . . . in November. And (*Sighs*) I think he's a

DISCUSSION

you and your husband fight a good deal about your not staying at home. Have you had an argument about this recently? Can you take us through such an argument?"

Part of the problem is that the themes of P.*8* were probably difficult to disentangle at the moment of exchange. On such an occasion, rather than fall back on a request for factual information, it may be useful to try to find some means for absorbing the communication. A statement such as P.*8* may be repeated aloud, or an elaboration of one aspect of it may be asked for, or the therapist may try to sift it silently in a long pause in order to get the feel of it.

T.*11:* The number and ages of the children, and "Mmmhnn," do not have the effect of expanding the glimpse of her life that P.*8* affords us. No doubt the person is resistant to bringing herself into focus. There is no evidence, however, that the resistance is unusually pronounced in her case. Even at this point it may well have yielded to involvement with vitalizing material.

T.*12:* A simple, direct effort to share in the person's mind and experience.

P.*12:* The person is about to shift the focus to her husband, insinuating he had deceived her before marriage by not letting her know what kind of person he was. Obviously this diverts attention from her, but if entered into concretely enough, it might not only describe him but also her as well, possibly casting some light on whether or not she could have had an inkling of the problem and on how she deals with it presently.

T.*13:* Again the therapist's response is to collect a fact.

P.*14:* The person goes right through the fact to establish her case. Note, however, that she "thinks" that her

INTERVIEW

chronic alcoholic. He drinks every day, and he just can't seem to let the stuff alone. He says he can, but he can't. He never has been able to except (*Sighs*) the one time the doctor had him on a diet (*Half-sigh*) and then he ate candy bars. Candy bars; I suppose he had to have sugar. But it's just (*Half-sigh*) I feel that it's . . . it's either going to ruin me or the kids or all of us. It . . .

T.*15:* What does he do?

P.*15:* He's a truck driver.

T.*16:* One of these long-distance hauls or what?

P.*16:* No. He used to do it. He doesn't now. They just do (*Sighs*) . . . ah . . . hauling within the state. And about (*Sighs*) mm . . . five or six months ago he went on trailers. Well I know it's hard, but he comes home and he takes it out on all of us. He starts nagging the minute he gets in the house.

T.*17:* Is he away a good deal?

P.*17:* (*Sighs.*) He eats and sleeps in the house, and that's all there is to it. And it's an insult to me naturally.

T.*18:* Mmmhnn. (*Short pause.*)

P.*18:* (*Sighs.*) Once in a while he's decent. (*Pause; sighs.*) I keep thinking of divorce, but (*Half-sigh*) that's another emotional death. And I don't want to do it with the kids right now. They're too young.

## DISCUSSION

husband is an alcoholic. As this and the rest of the statement suggests she is dealing primarily in her views and thoughts about things.

T.*15:* Another fact. Again the opportunity is lost to get into the scene, to see what really happens between husband and wife. The therapist might, for example, have asked: "How do you mean, ruin you? What sort of thing happens when he drinks. Has there been an incident about it, recently, yesterday or this week?"

P.*16:* Despite the diversion of having to develop peripheral information, the person returns to an area of difficulty, one which brings the session very close to her actual situation.

T.*17:* Thus a limited piece of information is solicited. The reconstruction of actual events could easily have been initiated in relation to P.*16* with a question such as: "Can you give me an example of his nagging?"

P.*17:* Having to respond only to circumscribed facts which do not activate her qualities, she is slowly being enveloped by a convenient cloud of thoughts and conceptions, very likely quite removed from the actualities. By P.*17* her thought-images are serving mainly to intensify a self-generated sense of being wronged.

P.*18:* Not just a thought, but a dramatic and purple one. Once in this cloud, she floats on to being even further removed from life by putting forward a disembodied idea about "divorce being an emotional death."

INTERVIEW

T.*19:* Divorce is an emotional death?

P.*19:* (*Sighs.*) I think so.

T.*20:* I don't quite understand what you mean. (*Short pause.*)

P.*20:* (*Sighs.*) Well it's . . . I think it's a . . . worse than death. If he died I think I'd be happy. I honestly would. (*Tearful.*)

T.*21:* Mmmhnn. I didn't understand.

P.*21:* (*Interrupting.*) And he won't get help. That's the trouble. He won't admit that it's any problem.

T.*22:* I would like to hear more about that, but first I . . . I didn't quite understand that about divorce being an emotional death.

P.*22:* (*Wearily.*) I don't know whether I can explain it. (*Sighs.*) (*Short pause.*)

T.*23:* Are you opposed to divorce . . . ah . . . generally or?

P.*23:* Yes, I am.

T.*24:* On what grounds?

P.*24:* (*Interrupting.*) That's why I'm here (*Smacks lips*) because I think a lot of marriages can be salvaged. (*Sighs; crying softly.*)

T.*25:* Now on what grounds are you generally opposed to divorce?

P.*25:* Well I think that the children . . .

T.*26:* Mmmhnn.

P.*26:* . . . are the ones who suffer really. It's still a stigma to divorce in our family. It's very strong.

(*Then follows a series of questions, much like the preceding ones, designed to explore the question of divorce, covering such items as religious background, possible moves in the future, and so forth. The person's remark in* P.*29—that in the event of divorce "it would be hard for*

DISCUSSION

P.*19:*   Notice that she is again dealing with thoughts.

T.*22:*   The therapist is trapped by the theme "divorce is an emotional death." It has a clinical flavor, it contains charged terms such as divorce, death, emotions, and the person is tearful at points while talking about it. It is judged to exceed in importance her claim that her husband is blind, stubborn, and insensitive. Susceptibility to thoughts leads to a lengthy exploration of the person's attitude toward a solution before the actual problem has been encountered.

T.*25:*   Such a question is likely to produce defensive opinions and ideas.

INTERVIEW

*me to readjust. It's hard enough now to keep my head above water"—is passed over.*)

P.*36:* But I'm still generally opposed to it . . .

T.*37:* Yes.

P.*37:* . . . because I think that . . . that I can be straightened out.

T.*38:* That you can be straightened out?

P.*38:* Yes.

T.*39:* I didn't get the impression that you thought it was . . . ah . . . your problem.

P.*39:* Well it's affecting me. It's making me unstable. I never used to be like this.

T.*40:* Yes?

P.*40:* Things didn't used to bother me this way. I used to be depressed. Occasionally. Sure! Who isn't? But not the way I am now. Not so that I wanted to turn on gas and jump out of the window.

T.*41:* How long have you been feeling that way? (*Clears throat.*)

P.*41:* Ever since I've been married. And on the honeymoon (*Voice breaks*) he drank every night. He didn't want to go anywhere. All he wanted to do was sit in and drink. And I couldn't see that.

DISCUSSION

P.*36–37:*   The futility of following this kind of material is thus summed up.

T.*39:*   Here the therapist practically remonstrates with the person. He says, in effect, you have been leading us a merry chase, blaming your husband, and now suddenly you acknowledge you have something to do with it! Reprimanded and challenged the person cannot elaborate P.*37* but finds refuge in some vague self-justification (P.*39*).

P.*40:*   The rebuke of T.*39* drives the person to say, in effect, don't be too hard on me, I really am in a bad way. She is unable to express this in personal terms, so instead she presents an official version of being badly off, the contemplation of suicide.

T.*41:*   The therapist is caught up by this psychopathological statement, but only momentarily. Material of this sort is often assumed to call for historical perspective and so we have the question of T.*41*. Since such a question brings her no closer to her present life, as might a question about what actually goes on between them at home, her answer is both unlikely and diversionary. She could not have been feeling like jumping out of the window ever since her marriage.

69

## DISCUSSION

The therapist is irritated with the person (T.39) largely, I think, because the interview is difficult for him. He resents following her into cul-de-sacs, yet he does not quite anticipate that this is where they are about to go. The frequency with which the exchange comes to a dead-end results mainly from the therapist's lack of clarity about what constitutes useful material. This lack of clarity leads to an implicit and irritable demand that the person just come out and own up to things. Yet surely the person is not aware that her course is one of evasion. The therapist's attitude is, in effect, a demand that the person take sole responsibility for the development of useful material, which is not only unrealistic but underestimates the contribution the clinician can make.

In terms of responding to material, the din of conventional clinical definitions has dulled this therapist's ear for person-to-person meanings. When he is not falling back on "facts," he is exploring ideas, views or clinical "red flags." On the question of what constitutes useful material, two categories of the person's statements may be compared. On the one hand, she says:

- I'm a nurse but my husband won't let me work.
- He says my place is home with the children.
- He nags me all the time.
- I need to get away from the children (once in a while).

On the other hand, she states:

- There are a lot of things I didn't know about him before marriage.
- I think he is an alcoholic.
- I keep thinking of divorce but that is death.
- It gets so bad I want to jump out of the window.

The therapist follows the statements of the first category only briefly and haltingly. Those in the second category are pursued more insistently. The theme of divorce is the most conspicuous example in the second category and is closely scrutinized from T./P.*18* through T./P.*38.* Yet the statements in the first category refer to situations that commonly occur in life; they are down-to-earth, they represent the kinds of things that can occur in any family. In contrast, the statements in the second category represent views rather than actualities, dramatic fantasies or psychopathological possibilities, which in psychotherapy, as in life, constitute diversions or escapes.

The detailed excerpts thus far are fairly representative of the general interaction that takes place in the course of the interview. In much of the remaining material the person gives her views of events, people, and history without developing detail about actual situations. For example, in P.*44,* after meandering indecisively about on the question of whether her husband is alcoholic, in the last few sentences she says she has to force her husband to spend time with the children. Rather than getting into what happens between father and children, through examples of situations and events, the therapist is carried along by the gist of her remarks and summarizes by saying:

T.*45:* He doesn't care for the children?

The person responds with a defensive illogic:

P.*45:* He apparently cares for them when he is with 'em, when he has to be with 'em. But that's all. He just doesn't seem to want to be bothered for any length of time. He comes home, he eats dinner, he reads his paper, and he falls asleep.

71

This statement then runs on at considerable length touching upon her husband's drinking, his allergies, the happiness of her family life compared to his, difficulties with the children, and so forth.

The excerpt from P.45 is a good illustration of the person seeming to talk about events but in fact giving only her version of events. That he doesn't "seem" to want to be bothered, that he comes home, reads his paper, and falls asleep, may be very different from what he actually did yesterday and the day before and the day before. Unchecked by actualities, she can cast these summaries in terms that protect her. One exception is the exchange (T./P.71–85) concerning her husband's objections to her not being home enough, which brings out her restlessness, possible lack of responsibility in relation to the children, and also the possibility that she does not find enough satisfaction in the children.

For the most part, there is in this interview such a paucity of material making for mutual and self-contact, that the therapist has to resort to catching her inconsistencies. In T.81, for example, he remarks that in view of what she has said about the husband, he hadn't expected to hear that the husband is concerned about who baby-sits with the children. Toward the end of the interview, probably as a result of the therapist having dealt with her resistance to some degree, of a certain down-to-earth interest and receptiveness on his part, of her desire to confess, and of a number of meaningful exchanges between therapist and person, she does acknowledge that she has had her problems in the past. She indicates that she has knocked around a good deal without having quite established a relationship with anyone, that she may have been indiscriminate, and had been pregnant through another man just before marriage. These events are acknowledged mainly as historical occurrences. They are not related to specific personality characteristics; the probability that these characteristics generate comparable problems in the present is hinted only vaguely. It is almost as if she confesses at the end she has been a "bad girl" but little is specified about her make-up as a person that tends to produce difficulties (e.g., she does not expect to be wanted, is not getting very much out of even intimate relationships, turns her back on problems, is accustomed to kicking around in a restless way, is not hoping for very much in life).

A general acknowledgment of problems, such as takes place in this interview, constitutes a commitment of sorts and is an achievement. Still, sharper definitions of characterological issues would have helped give this person a better sense of the work that has to be done.

The verbatim excerpts from this interview, together with the discussion and the summary of the direction eventually taken in the exchange, provide illustrations of the following points: a) some of the refinements of intellectuality to be found in clinical interviewing, b) certain of the standard assumptions that affect the initial interview, c) the distinction between vital and thought varieties of communication, and d) some means for developing material that might lend the interview an experiential cast.

# *Four*

# THE CASE HISTORY

*THE CASE HISTORY* is a staple fixture of clinical practice. After hearing about the difficulties that bring the person for consultation, many clinicians then initiate therapy by reviewing with the person the facts and major events of his life. The weight accorded the history is reflected also in the custom of beginning case supervision with the presentation of the history to the supervisor. Then, too, almost every case conference opens with the familiar and lengthy recital of the history.

The history is so respectably entrenched because it is

supposed to throw light, in Sullivan's words, on "one really pertinent question, [namely,] Who is this person and how does he come to be here?"[1] This is one of the continuously crucial questions of therapy and can therefore itself serve as the criterion of the usefulness of the case history. The history attempts to answer this question by surveying the conditions of a person's life, with particular emphasis on the experiences of the individual in various stages of his development. Large areas of the past are retraced in considerable detail: Infancy, Childhood, Puberty, Family Life, Education, Sex, Marriage, Vocational Record, and so on. This general plan of approach seems entirely reasonable, yet its very plausibility blankets a number of thorny issues.

What first leads to a reexamination of the history is the unadorned observation that it does not work as it is supposed to. In time one finds that the light cast by the history is limited and conjectural and that frequently the first version is supplanted later in therapy by a significantly different one. Furthermore, when one listens to a history without having seen the person, he is left with a sense of not having gotten to "know" the person. The person as reduced to some kind of conceptual order through the history, is often not recognizable in the flesh. Even on the level of etiologic order he is not encompassed by his sociohistorical framework. In some instances the person and the history as told are largely congruous; more often this is so only up to a point, for usually the individual emerges as more than or discontinuous with his history. In short, there is some question that the history serves decisively to illuminate the "Who" and "Why" of Sullivan's question.

1. Sullivan, *The Psychiatric Interview*, p. 141.

## A 'Typical' History

These issues may be made more concrete if the discussion is based on excerpts from a more or less typical history, selected from a series of case presentations. The excerpts are extensive enough to give a sense of the kind of data usually available in a history for forming a picture of an individual.

CASE HISTORY: JEAN B.

A. *Identifying data:* Age 29. Housewife. Lives in lower middle class development in Pennsylvania. Husband, Frank, age 33. There is one daughter, age 4½. Religion, Catholic.

B. *Presenting Problem:* Marital incompatibility. Frequent bitter fights. Husband unreasonable in demands for freedom re. hours at which he comes home and evenings out. Business matters more than family. Feelings of helpless rage in these disputes. Many fears—of being alone, of something happening to the baby, of interlopers who will assault her, etc. Difficulty in sleeping. Enormous tension about household routine. Poor interpersonal relations with neighbors. Many long-held grudges against husband's family. Many scars of early traumatic experiences. Difficulties centering on pre-menstrual tension, bad headaches, grinding teeth, vague aches and pains; phobic fantasies and dreams.

C. *History:* Middle child of 7. Five brothers, one sister. Mother frequently ill as was pt. during early years with stays in the hospital including those at births of two younger sons. Pt. was also sickly as a small child. Asthmatic.

Hospitalization for pneumonia followed by highly significant events—a stay at a Catholic convalescent home. This was pt's. first experience of order, routine, cleanliness, gentle voices, enough food, etc. Remembers particularly a reading hour in the afternoon. Though there were one or two painful episodes at the home—being falsely accused of something and never having the injustice acknowledged —these apparently were insufficient to mar the positive impression.

Illness, plus the hectic relations with parents and the even more unsettled period that followed the parents divorce when the pt. was about 10 resulted in lengthy periods when the pt. was not in school. Relationships with peers were negatively affected if only by the fact that the pt's. self-esteem at school was much injured. There was one brief semester when she made excellent progress with a sympathetic teacher, but this blossoming with the bit of warmth the teacher provided did not affect her self-concept because the class was one for slow learners. Peer relations were poor even into high school where the pt. was acutely aware of her mother's poor reputation and felt labeled by it, defensive even in the associations she did have.

After the divorce there were several people to whom she was sent successively. There were relatives of the mother or friends. The pt. felt that most of these people did not want her. In the home of one, sexual overtures were made to her on two or three occasions. After being returned to her mother pt.

was no longer sent away, but apparently existence was touch and go and full of trauma.

Mother worked but had men friends who gave her presents of money. Pt. remembers occasions when sleeping in bed with mother and mother's lover when they had intercourse. Has a vague but horror-filled memory of the man using the sink as a urinal (she thought the substance he passed semen) and her being compelled to clean the sink. She dates her own obsessive cleanliness about bathrooms to this memory. When pt. was in her teens mother broke down and tho the story is unclear here, was probably hospitalized. Pt. had to go to father leaving high school without graduating.

Relationships with father were always poor. Father is described as a small man, but pt. remembers him as very angry and dangerous. She recalls an incident when she was playing on the floor near him when she inadvertently got in his way and was shoved across the floor. She also recalled an incident not clearly remembered but very upsetting about his comment when she was very small and playing on the floor, about her pants showing, implying that she was showing her genitalia. When she was older, she felt that he expected she would be a tramp like her mother. This particular prediction she heard frequently from a number of people. When obliged to live with him pt. was no better able to live with him. He gave her no financial help at all so she worked in a dime store. After a while the situation became intolerable and she went to live with another aunt. Things went well at first but gradually worsened as the aunt's son became interested in the pt. and his mother grew antagonistic.

Meanwhile pt. had secured a job in a department store where she met her future husband. Both were attracted, she by his drive, the stability of his family background and by the hope of another life which he offered. Pt. did well at the store but could not cope with the flirtatious ways of employers and was unable to get along very well with the other girls. This discomfort and the miserable home situation drove her to marriage. The boy's parents disapproved so the couple eloped.

The twelve years of this marriage have been extremely hectic. Despite the fact it is a Catholic marriage, there has been through most of it a kind of uncertainty whether it will take as well as a constant return to a situation both parties experience as frustrating. A separation '54–'58, a year's residence in another state, experienced by the pt. as an exile. There was a separation of several months during pregnancy and another period of separation during 1961.

Separation during '61 less formal. Husband had room away. Pt. suspicious, fearful of actually losing him. Possibly under pressure of final break-up of marriage—in any case—experienced satisfaction in sex relation after having been extremely averse since birth of daughter. Following this experience was a visit to Planned Parenthood Federation, made with great inner conflict partly about the issue of having another child. She and her husband both want a baby, but pt. concerned that she may not be able to handle two tiny children. Also the marriage was in so unstable a state that the burden of another child would make it even harder for her to leave her husband and maintain herself. Another source of conflict had to do with the genital examination which disgusted pt. and aroused much anxiety.

Another crisis during summer of '62 in which the pt. very distraught. Cause of crisis not known. Since this occasion crisis abated, much less intense. Relationship with neighbors less traumatic. More satisfactions and communication between husband and wife since then—except in sex area.

If we attempt, on the basis of this history to say who this person is, we find very little that marks out a particular person. The data has to be strained to produce a characterization and in so doing we are pushed to rather flimsy conjectures. One fact alone suggests that this difficulty would be inevitable: Such a history is not rare, yet in actuality it can give rise to very different kinds of individuals. How could one have predicted from this material that the person in question has a chip on her shoulder, has little tolerance for challenge, does not get much done in daily life, cannot handle ordinary ups and downs, finds it hard to take being wrong, experiences difficulties as assaults upon her, deals with impotence and fear with an armor of anger? At the same time what comes through any contact with her is that her pain remains alive, is real and raw, and that her anger is as much fight to endure as it is ire per se. There is also about her a certain concern for fairness, a resourcefulness, and a steadfastness about trying to improve her life. (Indeed recent contact indicates that this person has carried through significant changes of personality.)

The chances are small that the history material would have enabled anyone to describe her explicitly in these terms. Yet if one listens to the recording of even a single therapeutic session with her, much of this picture is readily available. It is most instructive in one's work or in case conferences to compare the sense of person that emerges from the study of history material to that which comes through almost any form of direct experience of the individual.

It may be objected that this history did not include a section on the clinician's impressions of the person. This was omitted deliberately to emphasize what we actually draw on to answer the question, "Who is this person?" On this score the sociohistorical conditions of a person's life are relatively uninformative. In taking a history it is easy to become confused about which categories of data actually provide the portrait of the person. Although the process involves a concentration on conditions of the past, the person is, at the same time, being met directly and also is being seen in action in certain situations he describes. It is essentially through this direct experience, rather than the data of the past that we learn who the person is. Past conditions may suggest certain possible realms of difficulty, but they do not define qualitatively the identity of the person.

## Questions About the Case History Method

A great deal is involved in getting to know a person, little of which is acknowledged or emphasized explicitly in the case history method. In the general method of which history-taking is a part, the contact begins with a review of symptoms or characteristics; these are then related to etiologic factors identified in the social development of the

person; and the person is then regarded as "understood."
Thus the question "Why" comes into the foreground very
early; "Who" apparently is presumed to have been answered. Because the answer to the question "Who" requires
time and a particular type of interaction, this methodology
leaves us in the hasty position of trying to account for a
person before we really know what has to be accounted
for. The study of the past may suggest certain problems or
even qualities the person is likely to have, but people are
affected so variously by the conditions of their development that direct experience of the person remains the only
sure way of defining the issues of the work. This is not to
suggest that knowledge of historical conditions is irrelevant; learning about the past is obviously of value in understanding the person. The concern in this discussion is
rather with the conditions under which this is best done—
that is, with procedure, timing, and effectiveness.

The early set to find causes, to explain, has numerous
effects; in particular it tends to intellectualize the therapeutic contact. The person's history becomes a backdrop
on which the therapist tries to sketch in certain theories
and principles. Connections derived from these theories are
drawn between certain social conditions (parental attitudes, toilet training, childhood traumas, and so on) and
current problems or characteristics. In this activity higher
thought processes such as reasoning and inference tend to
predominate.

Consider, for example, the case of a therapist who hears
from a person that she has difficulty with her children—is
unable to stay with them very long and when with them is
more impatient than she should be. In reviewing her history the therapist learns she has been brought up by the

maternal grandparents, though her own parents lived only a block away. Following prevailing theory it was very easy for the therapist to settle on an hypothesis of rejection, which he maintained for some time and which got in the way of his seeing the person clearly. As it happens the person was brought up by the grandmother not because of rejection on the mother's part, but because psychologically the mother was herself too infantile to bring up a child. The problem was not so much lack of love as it was that the only love the person has known is the love available to a baby.

The point here is not to debate psychodynamics or to argue the possibility that this state of affairs would have been detected by a keener clinician; rather it is to suggest that the case-history methodology encourages the use of analytic-inferential-deductive processes and that whatever the caliber of the clinician these methods tend to impair contact with the person. If this person's complaint were not at the outset taken as a problem that has to be explained conceptually, if she could have been experienced as a "baby" (which is itself an explanation), therapy might have been more realistic. All that was needed to start off on the right track was to be moved by the slight childlike whine in her voice, but this can happen only when one is oriented to absorb rather than explain. Clinicians are too often swept along by the history methodology, which involves making the person explicable by applying principles and formulating ideas that intellectually bridge the gap between his problems and his past. Some of these ideas may well be applicable in certain instances. What is being challenged is not the content of the ideas, but the effectiveness of the approach in relation to its own objectives. In any event, knowing does not begin with ideas; indeed, in knowing, ideas only cap the process. There is a major phase of knowing in which one does not explicitly seek to develop hypotheses or apply principles, but attempts rather to absorb and be affected by the material.

The case history method also involves the person being interviewed in such a way as to likewise impair the whole process of knowing. The person is asked to tell about conditions, persons, or events in his past; he is asked, in effect, to describe, identify, search his memory (recall), summarize or tell what he thinks (give his view). Thus he is encouraged to employ essentially intellectual processes as a basis for making himself known, which presents a narrow and shallow field for contact. In such activity he excites only a few of his own senses and even fewer of the listener's. The history depends largely on intellectual reports of conditions, which can give the therapist an opportunity to try out his theories, but under these circumstances both person and therapist bring only very limited aspects of themselves into play.

*Searching Out History*

There is, of course, a history for each person, but it will be missed if it is pursued as "The History." Above all, history is always individual, and questions about the past have to be put in particular ways and in proper season. This is the state of affairs to which the clinician has to defer. Only if the clinician fails to realize that it is the person alone who can bring us to remote corners of his mind and heart will these questions be asked at the beginning of therapy.

At the inception of therapy the person almost by definition is not ready for such clarity and penetration. There is too much he would rather not know or has not the resources to know. Like most people he still has a major stake in seeing his life in some palatable form. People enter therapy with comprehensive theories of how they came to be what they are and with equally definite notions of just how therapy should be done. Given these conditions, our guide often conducts a tour of sights long familiar and even welcome to him. A competent clinician may be able on occasion to reroute this tour so as to catch more significant glimpses of the past, but just as often this is hard to do. The person's energies can more effectively be taken up with laying the groundwork for being in touch with himself, with developing meaningful communication, and with improving psychological resources and integration. These factors are essential to any effective exploration of the past.

Even with the best intentions it is very difficult to see the past in the present. Numerous studies have demonstrated unequivocally (a result not often achieved in formal psychological research) the poor correspondence of mothers' reports of developmental events and child-rearing practices with what actually transpired during their children's earlier years.[2] Writing of the difficulties encountered in

2. M. K. Pyles, H. R. Stoltz, J. W. MacFarlane, "The Accuracy of Mothers' Reports on Birth and Developmental Data," *Child Development,* VI (1935), pp. 165–176. Ernest A. Haggard, Arne Breckstad, Åse Gruda Skard, "On the Reliability of the Anamnestic Interview," *Journal of Abnormal and Social Psychology,* LXI (1960), pp.

surveying his own history, Einstein asks whether the past one sees at the age of 20 is the same that will be seen at 30 or 50 or 67. "Every reminiscence," he writes, "is colored by today being what it is and therefore by a deceptive point of view. . . . Nevertheless," he stresses, "much can be lifted out of one's own experience which is not open to another consciousness."[3]

Perhaps the largest problem in evaluating past experience is that the past is so vast and complex a domain. It is distantly dotted with people and events exerting important effects both subtle and obvious, all having to be seen with a light that varies with maturational and characterological conditions. Einstein sees further difficulty arising from "the manifoldness of the external situations and the narrowness of the momentary content of consciousness [which] bring about a sort of atomizing in the life of every human being."[4] The task of picking out of this intricate tangle the vital and determining strands of a person's development might well give pause even to the most intrepid.

In prospecting such territory it is only human to wish one had a map, and this is precisely what the history attempts to supply. Built into the history in effect is an etiologic outline. One searches the past for the factors and conditions generally associated (depending upon one's orientation) with difficulties in living. This is typical case-

311–318. Charles Wenar, "The Reliability of Mothers' Histories," *Child Development*, XXXII (1961), pp. 491–500.

3. Albert Einstein, "Autobiographical Notes," in *Albert Einstein: Philosopher-Scientist*, ed. P. A. Schilpp (Evanston, Ill.: Library of Living Philosophers, 1949), p. 3.

4. *Ibid.*, p. 7.

history procedure, the value of which is affirmed explicitly by Sullivan. According to him the history rests on a "some schematization of the way people, under the most fortunate circumstances, come to be as capable and human as they are."[5] Sullivan's schematization involves a description of the developmental interpersonal experiences he regards as essential to psychological well-being. Against this framework one is able to identify deficiencies of experience which become "the principal business of the psychiatrist."[6]

Possession of a map may be reassuring, but it is a basic law of touring that the more one studies the map, the less one sees of the landscape. One may get neatly from one place to another, but one is not likely to roam round long enough to make discoveries. In individual therapy this is the kind of activity that counts. Too often these maps give the illusion that there are standard paths over psychological terrain. But no two people ever present the same terrain; these etiologic maps are at once too limited and too general to offer more than a probabilistic understanding of a person.

Areas difficult to reach are naturally poorly represented in history schemas. Most of them have very little to say about the problem of native endowment, yet the case history rests, as Sullivan has indicated, on the proposition that the individual is a product of his past experiences and his endowment. For all its axiomatic flavor the interaction between experience and endowment remains poorly defined. In what ways does endowment affect the meaning of particular events to the individual? Is a screechy mother harder on a finely tempered child than on one of rougher

5. Sullivan, *The Psychiatric Interview*, p. 140.
6. *Ibid.*, p. 147.

grain? Indeed what events are created by endowment per se. A child may have no particular problem beyond being highly physical and expressive, but his activity may just happen to exceed his mother's tolerance for problems and clatter. This combination may very well set in motion a negative and perhaps serious chain of events. Another child in the same family, quiet, contemplative, may have quite a different experience with the mother and the mother with him.

In the history there tends to be far more data on how the world affected the person than on what kind of factor he was in relation to the world. Histories are flavored by this kind of externalism; the forces we get to know about are those that act upon the person (parents, siblings, neighborhood, traumatic events). This is a general problem in therapy, but one much accentuated in regard to the past, because the younger one is, the more limited the capacity to see oneself affecting one's own life.

Considerations of this kind lead one to wonder whether it is really possible to unravel the past. Even after years of contact with a person I have been left doubtful that the history assembled was truly complete. There are, of course, important data to be gleaned from the past, but these data are fractional and limited in their explanatory power, though none the less valuable for this. Fortunately it has yet to be demonstrated that etiological explanations such as are developed by means of case history material are crucial to therapy. In therapy, experiencing who one is seems more basic to change than states of intellectual coherence, which is a large part of the value of linking the past with the present.

The issues and areas associated with any case history

scheme usually mark out significant realms of experience. Certain ones, such as parental relationships, are of prime importance in the formation of personality. The clinician surely needs to be familiar with the concepts associated with such categories, but this is to be distinguished from the problem of how to study these areas in the individual. General agreement on the importance of a category has led to attempts to gather information quickly and directly about such areas. A clinician may learn a good deal from asking what the father is like, but I find there is more to be learned from some specific incident that occurs between person and father. Events of everyday life contain data bearing on most of the usual categories of the history, but in the form of fresh experiences rather than cognitive summaries or recollections. Furthermore, much can be learned about the conditions of the past in the present. A son, looking on during an exchange between his mother and father, notices a slashing cruelty in his mother when her needs are not considered first. He may well discover in such a moment how he happened to learn in the past to defer to the wishes of others by blanking out his own. The past is part of the present just as the present is part of the future.

The search of the past calls for an effective degree of integration and relative objectivity on the part of the searcher. Even if this is available there is such a large expanse to look over that one must strike a direction. The direction can be established by a theoretical map or, preferably, it can be determined by the actualities of the person. Once it is known and clear that the person has this or that compelling characteristic, it is much easier to single out relevant aspects of the past. When one knows what one is trying to account for, when one is interested in and capable of sustaining the truth, then the search of the past becomes a venture at once more difficult and more rewarding.

# Five

# INTERPRETATION

*IN THE* general scheme that has grown out of the psychoanalytic tradition, therapy begins with the initial interview, is followed by a survey of the person's life (history), and then is suceeded by an extended phase in which the major objective is for the person to come to know himself. The chief tool available to the therapist in implementing this end is assumed to be interpretation.

Interpretation is directed toward the development of insight—that is, toward enabling the person to see into and understand himself. As an approach it has an immediate, commonsense appeal; if one knows what is amiss in a situation, one is in a better position to remedy it. Elaborate philosophical and scientific approaches have been floated on this sturdy kernel only to run aground. Socrates, who defined virtue as knowledge, held that "knowledge is a commanding thing . . . and will not allow a man, if only he knows the difference of good and evil, to do anything which is contrary to knowledge."[1] He learned the hard way not to underestimate the complications besetting the uses of knowledge, and we in therapy have been learning the same lesson, though at considerably less cost. Clinical experience has jarred the old faith in the simple efficacy of self-knowledge. As a result psychologists have been compelled to approach again and again the problem of what is self-knowledge, under what conditions does it develop, and how does such knowledge affect a person's life.

### The Model of Medicine

Despite its significant function in generating self-knowledge, interpretation is by no means a well-defined procedure. Even today therapists of different persuasions disagree over what should be interpreted and in what way. In the history of psychotherapy there is considerable room for these differences, for interpretation did not spring full-blown as a therapeutic activity but gradually acquired its meanings in a series of contexts.

During the latter half of the nineteenth century psychotherapy took a great leap forward, the momentum of which

1. *The Works of Plato*, trans. Benjamin Jowett (New York: The Dial Press, 1936), IV, p. 193.

has carried to the present day. As a field involving the lives of people, it was naturally affected by the philosophical, intellectual, and scientific climate of the time. Most immediately, however, psychotherapy was modeled on the methods of medicine; in fact its early concepts were formulated mainly by physicians. Medicine's impressive advances in the field of physical disorders rested on a particular systematic finding, namely, that physical disorders tend to manifest themselves in relatively consistent groupings of signs and that these groupings (and therefore the disorder) are determined by one or several specific factors. In diphtheria or appendicitis, for example, a direct connection was established between the illness, particular symptoms, and a specific underlying physical factor. Symptoms were thus legitimately regarded as significant leads to the nature of the disease itself. This principle established a pattern of approach to the study and treatment of physical disorders. It led to the careful study of symptoms, to efforts to classify these symptoms, to attempts to relate groupings to an underlying cause, which then became the focus of treatment. Medical practice was organized about the findings of these researches and involved the identification of symptoms and the application of pre-existing knowledge concerning the connection between specific symptoms and specific causes. Further refined, for the individual physician it is a process of recognizing and keeping in mind significant signs, discarding superficialities, then matching the signs to a series of conceivably relevant causes known to have such effects.

Psychotherapists followed closely the productive course taken by medicine. People were (and still are) carefully studied in terms of their presenting symptoms. Efforts were made to group these signs into a systematic nosology.

Guides for the observation of behavior were provided by Kraeplin, Bleuler, and others. The field proceeded on the faith that accurate classification would lead to the identification of separate disorders, which would then be differentiated in terms of distinct causes. Freud too voiced the belief that "the regular elements in the composition of the various forms of neurosis" would sooner or later be defined.[2] Although psychoanalysis broke with medicine at many points, in significant respects it remained under the sway of medical methodology, developing its own classificatory system based on symptomatology. The hallmarks, for example, of the neurosis (considered at the time the primary form of psychological disturbance) was the presence of certain typical symptoms such as unaccountable impulses, sensations, paralyses, or anxiety spells. The general category of neurosis consisted of a number of different types of disorders—anxiety neurosis, hysteria, obsessional neurosis, and so forth—each presumably distinguished from the other by different symptoms and etiology. Shortly, however, the early workers began to encounter disturbances lacking the classical symptoms of neurosis, whereupon they assumed they had come upon a new class of disorders, which they designated as the character disorders.

A moderately comprehensive system of classification was thus developed, but contrary to what one would anticipate, the various categories were accounted for in terms of the same cause—namely, some disturbance of the instincts, primarily of the libido. Although it is conceivable that all psychological difficulties are rooted in the disturbances of a single factor and that these disturbances simply appear in different forms, this view is itself an exception to medical

2. Freud, *Collected Papers*, II, p. 288.

methodology. Differentiation is not undertaken with the expectation that one cause will account for all differences. Classification characteristically has fared badly in relation to psychological difficulties, but the implications of this fact have not yet been fully accepted.

The earnest effort to implement the medical model met with difficulty at every turn. In regard to symptoms, for example, not only was the principle of method implicit in the model hard to apply, it was even difficult to hold fast to the medical meaning of the term. When the early analysts came upon disconcerting cases, the character disorders, that lacked typical symptoms, they were hard put to distinguish symptoms from personality characteristics. Personality in character disorders, writes Fenichel, is not relatively "uniform" (as he claims it is in the neurosis) but rather "torn" or "deformed" so that "one cannot say at what point the 'personality' ends and the 'symptom' begins."[3]

The concept of character disorder, in my view, was really not so much an addition to nosology as a correction of the concept of neurosis. Because the concept implied the axiomatic relationship of psychological difficulties to specific characteristics of personality, it was the first step toward relegating symptoms to a minor position. Even today it is perhaps not superfluous to ask whether the "hebephrenic" patient is in some fashion silly and incoherent by character, the more so when out of control. These manifestations are probably more characterological in one sense or other (imitative, acting out of incompetence, and so on) than symptomatic. The large sociocharacterological com-

3. Otto Fenichel, *The Psychoanalytic Theory of Neurosis* (New York: W. W. Norton, 1945), p. 18.

ponents involved in the production of symptoms probably have even greater significance than is generally appreciated. Within the last fifteen years we have witnessed the quiet disappearance of a large category of psychopathology, the manic-depressive psychoses, without preventative treatment having been applied to this "illness." Evidence is accumulating that the vast amount of effort expended on the meticulous classification of symptoms has been for naught.[4] At this point a growing number of clinicians regard symptoms, strictly defined (for example, tics, obsessions, insomnia), as the creakings of an entire personality under stress, not crucially or necessarily meaningful, except as a signal that something is amiss. If there are symptoms, and they seem to be fewer in number these days, they usually lead to general issues (parental relationships, modes of functioning, need satisfactions) with which we work in any case, whether or not symptoms are present.

4. An interesting light is cast on the psychological "syndromes" in a profile on Pilgrim State Hospital, "Pilgrim's Progress" by Morton M. Hunt, appearing in *The New Yorker* magazine of September 30, 1961. In the course of describing to the reporter the revolution in hospital care that followed the introduction of the tranquilizers, Dr. Henry Brill, director of the hospital, draws the reporter's attention to a case which he says turns up only very rarely in hospitals nowadays: "What I wanted you to see though is his rigidity. This is catatonia—a classical pattern that used to appear frequently in schizophrenics. Now it is mysteriously becoming very rare and we hardly see it anymore. The same thing is true of the manic type . . . and the old-style hallucinating psychotic. . . . All these clear-cut entities that have been seen and described plainly for generations are fading away. How do you explain it? Drugs? Well, yes, but only in part; it's not quite that simple. I suspect that general mental patients are strongly imitative and after they arrive here they tend to copy what other patients are doing. But nowadays we break up the symptoms so quickly that there isn't much for them to imitate." (pp. 60, 65)

Some of the efforts to preserve the symptom—cause proto-type strained ingenuity, but clinicians were equal to the challenge. A variation of the concept of symptoms was retained, for instance, by extending (and thereby altering) the meaning of the term. A view developed in which almost all aspects of personality were considered to be symptoms in effect—that is, derivatives or secondary consequences of an underlying factor. Passivity in a man, for example, might be taken simply as a reflection of the predominance of feminine libidinal currents, growing out of desire to copulate with the father. A trait such as passivity, however, is usually more than a sign; it has little of the superficial, temporary, derived, secondary character of symptomatology. Yet if we take up passivity as a durable, first-order issue, one that in its own right is the probable source of many difficulties, we are told we are up on the surface, not dealing with the fundamentals, not working in depth.

There are then in psychology, as in medicine, concepts in the category of sufficient cause. In addition reciprocals are taken for granted in psychology, just as in medicine; thus, for example, depression means repressed hostility and paranoia implies homosexuality. In medicine, however, causes and correlations are determined empirically and also apply consistently to the same set of conditions. Although psychotherapists are equally concerned about establishing relationships empirically, the format breaks down over the difficulty in finding consistent conditions of application. Following an empirical path, psychotherapists sought and discovered significant determinants in individual cases. Thereafter, the systematic guides of the medical model encouraged the belief that these findings could be directly applied to others. Accurate findings (probably only individual or partial in import), in combination with the assumptions of the medical model, have frequently in psychology, led to overgeneralizing and overweighting the significance of findings.

## The Medical Model and Interpretation

It is perhaps useful to detail further how the format of known cause and predetermined meanings (correlations) affects interpretation. Whatever is regarded as an accurate description or explanation of a particular reality, as fact or truth, inevitably orders the mind in approaching this reality. Confronted with a disorder, established knowledge usefully organizes the thinking of the physician. In psychotherapy reliance on "established knowledge" has similarly comprehensive effects. To begin with it predetermines the content of interpretation. If self-knowledge is the goal of interpretation, then established facts and truths define *what* must be communicated to the person. A postulated central cause, for example, determines, as it should if true and general, one's fundamental comprehension of a person and thus ultimately the content of the therapist's communications and interpretations.

A case in point is Fenichel's description of a woman whose problem is that her sexual aim includes the wish to be beaten. From the standpoint of classical psychoanalytic theory, not unexpectedly, her problem is seen as originating in the conflict revolving about the instinctual requirement to satisfy libidinal Oedipal wishes with her father. The gap between her wish to be beaten and the root condition is bridged as follows: Patient loved father, a misogynist, who preferred sister; father forbade anal-erotic practices of any kind; father disliked daughter because of her lack of penis; instinct demanded, however, that patient learn to endure her father's severity and contempt without ccasing to love him; so she becomes a masochist, with the sexual aim of being beaten; the penis, offensive to her, is replaced by the beating hand; father's behavior involving severity and contempt thus serves to satisfy her masochistically distorted Oedipal wishes.[5] The thread that accounts for every manifestation in this person is libidinal. The person loves father (no matter what he is like) because instinct demands it, the daughter is disliked because she lacks a penis, through masochism she secretly satisfies her Oedipal wishes. These are not empirically demonstrated correlations. No one has established that misogynists typically dislike women because they lack penises or that daughters remain bound to fathers mainly to satisfy libidinal instincts. Such "correlations" are developed on the basis of reductive chains of logic, starting from an assumption of the established explanatory power of a particular factor. Questions are thus resolved by developing reasonable or plausible connections to an underlying cause not by reference to demonstrated correlations. Logic is not as limiting as fact and in consequence such formulations are vulnerable to logical challenge. In this case, for instance, how does the misogynist manage to prefer the sister who, after all, is also lacking a penis? Might not the person's masochism reflect self-contempt or helplessness or demoralization as readily as instinctual urge? A few demonstrated correlations would dispose of such debate in short order, as they do in relation to run-of-the-mill physi-

5. Fenichel, pp. 362–363.

cal disorders. Despite his allegiance to empiricism the clinician functioning in this mode often turns out to be more logician than empiricist.

Established knowledge not only defines the content of what the person needs to learn about himself, but also determines *how* the varied phenomena of personality are to be met and understood. Established knowledge acts as a direction finder, drawing a straight line between question and answer. When the line appears to curve or spiral, it is often in therapeutic theory straightened out with an application of reasoning. These same points could be illustrated in any other theoretical system in which propositions of comprehensive generality are asserted. Strict adherence to the notion, for instance, that every difficulty has an interpersonal root, is bound to result in missing significant *intra*personal determinants. Even so limited a formula as the view that depression involves repressed hostility, predetermines what the clinician will search for and focus upon. If such operations were functional in therapy, the activities of the physician and psychotherapist would indeed be comparable. Comprehension of disorders would be a matter of recognizing signs that have certain set meanings. Yet this approach has only limited application in psychotherapy. It founders, in particular, on the rock of individuality.

Psychological meanings are at once more variable and unique than the meanings of physical phenomena. In medicine even signs seldom encountered tend to have the same meaning in different people. In psychology, however, even as common a sign as anger may well have dissimilar meanings in different individuals. In one person anger may be an attempt to intimidate, in another an expression of impotence, in another simply an appropriate reaction. Etiological considerations seem to have a similar systematic character. In the history of a brisk, emphatic, but basically uncertain person, one may find a mother who took over for him in general and especially whenever he ran into difficulty. Although this is a meaningful concurrence in this instance, there is no assurance that it will apply to another person with comparable characteristics. In the latter, such characteristics may be related to having been criticized too sharply whenever he made a mistake (and to a dozen other factors as well).

Although this type of knowledge does not afford the psychologist a general correlation, it is nevertheless valuable to him in affirming the lawful, determined nature of psychological functioning within the individual and in pointing toward what tends to be important in personality development. The accumulation of such findings provides the clinician with a compass, but not a path; such findings enable clinicians to get their bearings more quickly and to move more sure-footedly. Knowledge in psychology has its uses but not necessarily in the mode set by its methodological predecessors. Concepts are, of course, indispensable to psychology, but individuality supersedes generality, and the clinician has to be ready to subordinate any concept to his sense of things. Knowledge, in this field, has to be finely moderated by sense, feeling and continuous experience in applying the concepts of pychology. On this basis, fresh variations of knowledge develop not encompassed by the formal concepts themselves. As a result, concepts are more readily translated into activities (and therapy consists not of the discussion of ideas but of actions) which have application to individuals.

Even the mode of developing meanings differs for psychology and medicine. The meanings of physical phenomena do not emerge from immediate experience, rather they are defined in terms of their effects. A heart murmur heard for the first time has no inherent meaning; only long-term observation of its consequences establishes its significance. In the psychological realm meanings inhere in the experience itself. A child is frozen by harshness the first time he meets it; he doesn't have to meet it again and again to know what happened to him. Indeed children are often artlessly clear about rather complex qualities that they encounter in other persons. Similarly a therapist meeting for the first time an idiosyncrasy of speech—a momentary hesitation, a slight gulp, a brief working of the lips—has the experience of a person bottled up in some fashion, intimidated, who has to watch and censor what he says. Consider again the brisk person mentioned earlier. Despite his emphatic manner one can sense an uncertain sliding from one alternative to another; one becomes aware of being ingeniously maneuvered into advising on a choice of alternatives. Such apprehension does not necessarily involve the application of prior knowledge; it does not have the character of correlative, associative operations. If one is properly in touch with the person, one can experience the "disease" (meanings) without lengthy observational checks of effects.

Comprehension of psychological events requires an untrammeled play of all the psychologic systems of the interpreter. In the framework of set knowledge, the therapist's energies do not play freely upon the qualities of the individual, to flow wherever they may lead, to whatever shapes, magnitudes, connections, or roots they may have. Sooner or later this play is short-circuited as the therapist busies himself with converting the manifestation into a derivative of a cause or the reciprocal of another factor. Psychological apprehension involves, for definite periods, experiencing rather than thinking, immersion rather than observation, receiving rather than applying, combining rather than analyzing, unselfconsciousness rather than awareness, and in general a free play of sense, feeling, and intellect. Medical apprehension does not exclude the use of these systems, but as a matter of emphasis it depends more on ordered observational-associative-intellectual processes. The very mode of apprehension demanded of psychotherapists, it is worth noting, is so intimately attuned to the person that the issue of individuality is automatically taken into account.

Were psychological knowledge as generally applicable as medical knowledge, there would be no need for interpretation. Indeed the more therapists work from a base of established knowledge, the more their interpretations become a variety of explication. Although it is widely practiced, this kind of interpretation is looked down upon by therapists. On some level it is appreciated that the "explanatory" interpretation is the perquisite of relatively certain and general knowledge—conditions that do not sum up the character of useful psychological knowledge. It was not by chance that medicine adopted the term diagnosis rather than interpretation to cover its operations of comprehension. Obviously, in contrast, the term interpretation was impressed into service by psychotherapists out of some sense of its applicability. It may be worthwhile, then, to look into the meaning of the term, to open up its intimations of applicability, because implicit in the term may be guides for making more effective use of interpretation.

### Definitions of Interpretation

*Webster's New International Dictionary,* in its own fashion an invaluable psychological text, lists three denotations to the term *interpretation.* The first is to explain or tell the meaning of. This definition does not suffice for psychotherapy; every interpretation contains some element of explanation (or statement of meaning), but not every explanation is an interpretation. Crucial to the concept of interpretation, as Webster's remaining denotations suggest, is the question of how one arrives at knowledge as opposed to what one does with it (explains). With the accent in therapy so much on interpretation as explanation, it is often overlooked that interpretation involves a special form of apprehension as well as special ways of imparting this apprehension. To interpret, continues Webster, also means "to understand or appreciate in light of individual belief, judgment or interest; construe" and lastly, "to apprehend and represent by means of art." Taken by itself the first definition of interpretation can include the transmission of authoritative knowledge and information, and yet precisely this is excluded by the last two denotations. What approach to knowledge then renders even explanation an interpretation? The answer to this question has to begin with a description of the conditions that characteristically call for interpretation as the basis for developing understanding.

Interpretation has utility in situations where things are

not black or white and meanings are not fixed or arbitrary; where the many factors that combine to produce effects are difficult to rank in significance; and where there are few absolutes, ultimate standards, or final causes. Such a situation obtains, for example, in works of art, where there are no expectations of fixed meanings. Every apple in a series of still-lifes is not just another apple. Although there are factors common to all painting (form, color, perspective, movement, technique, sensibility, aesthetics), these may be uniquely combined so as to create dimensions of meaning that go beyond the factors or the objects represented. One artist, out of special comprehension and skill, affords a glimpse of the meaning of serenity in his representation of a human figure. Another compounds the same factors in such a way as to bring out instead the vitality of the body. We never know in advance of viewing a painting what we will find or learn. As for the value of a painting, we find that, beyond a certain level of competency and artistic maturity, it makes little sense to say one is truer or better than another. Titian is not superfluous because we have a Rembrandt. Nor are we able to define, technically or psychologically, the optimal combination of factors productive of great art. Even in relation to simple elements, one artist uses form to achieve remarkable effects; another creates experiences through light and shadow. Moreover, it is difficult to separate the significance of the factors; form affects color and color may create form; the factors are both separate and merged. For all these reasons the potential variation in outcomes remains forever infinite. This suggests that we will never have a "final" painting, which means that interpretation in this realm will never be supplanted by authoritative, established knowledge.

The situation in relation to human beings seem comparable in major respects. Human behavior reflects great variation; these variations are not easily read and certainly their meanings are not fixed. The meaning of the mating call may be unmistakable in certain species, but in the human being it may express anything from a desire to conquer to the wish to be cuddled or protected. We need only look around to see that infinitely varied combinations of human factors are possible. Again, providing that qualities do not reflect maldevelopment, it is hard to claim that one combination is better or truer than another. Not many would be persuaded that steadiness and penetration are fundamentally superior to vivaciousness and imaginativeness. The combination of all of these qualities is an outcome to be wished for, but it comes about only rarely; the French have thus made the most of reality with the phrase, *"vive la différence."* In any event, human psychology has all the marks of a domain that calls for interpretation as the approach of choice.

## A Standard of Significance

If responsibility for deciding what is important in each person's case devolves inescapably upon clinician and person, if preconceived, authoritative knowledge is not a sufficient guide to what is important (uniqueness is not to be found in a book), how then are we to direct our search for the significant? We need a touchstone at once exacting but not limiting. Such a guide is contained in the query: "Who is this person? What is he?" questions Sullivan and others constantly used to get their bearings. Although seemingly simple, the degree to which these questions are answered tests the significance of the description of a person. The question "Who and what am I?" is for each person perhaps the ultimate issue. It is not by chance that self-justification is so great a force in life and therapy. Even sanity rests upon the answer to this question. The escape in insanity is precisely away from an identity, a sense of self, that has become unendurable, so that one becomes someone or something else, a Napoleon, a fool, a vegetable.

When the clinician asks "Who is this person?" he is not asking for age or social status. Rather the clinician is asking what makes him the person he is, what is his uniqueness. Although *who* is frequently difficult to distinguish from *what* in relation to persons, answers to each of these interrogatives make its own contribution to the total picture. When the clinician speaks of human nature in general, he may ask *"What* is man?" but not *"Who* is man?" In relation to a particular individual, however, to ask *what* without *who* is to lose something. *Who* is *what* individualized. *What* is concerned with the more purely descriptive, with the parts and nature of personality, with what a person is made up of and how the "familiar" dimensions of personality work in him. In the exploration and description of personality we have to go along describing the components of a nature without knowing what we will come to. But *who* reminds us that the *whats* must eventually combine to make up a person. As we know better and better *what* a person is the *who* emerges effortlessly. The inclusive question *"Who* and *what* are you?"* provides an alternative to the customary orientation of being sent to observe the operations of the libido or of security systems or of drives for mastery. A person is more than any or all of these things. This question can direct our search precisely because it is involved with the notion of person. Implicit in the concept of person (the general sense of the human being evolved over ages of experience) are standards of individuality, actuality, comprehensiveness, depth, which if met are likely to render descriptions meaningful.

*Who* also adds to *what* a dimension of comparative appreciation by asking, in effect, what kind of person are you, what have you become? Taken in combination, these interrogatives lead to descriptions that are, in effect, measures of a person's condition. Adjectives such as *frightened, egocentric, forceful, demanding, intense, alert,* and *glib,* define characteristics that are also indicators of a person's current psychological status. In combination they represent an outcome. In thus describing *who* and *what,* we are defining the issues of the work and also are being provided with guides for further exploration. Glibness, for example, has a character that will in the course of the work suggest the relevance of certain factors rather than others. Guided by characteristics and meaning, we explore the combination of factors and experience that make for a particular outcome.

This general position has a number of implications for interpretation. It challenges the degree to which theory is allowed to determine the direction and content of interpretation. Any meaningful theory or concept may take shape as an issue in a particular person, but the contrary is just as likely. Even when certain concepts are affirmed in a particular individual, they tend either to vary in some unique fashion or to be linked with and modified by others of equal significance. In the break with the concept of basic cause and with the assumption of fixed psychodynamic

110

meanings, arbitrary priorities tend to be washed out. Consider again the person whose mother intervened whenever things were difficult and who now hangs back and avoids situations in which he may have to try himself out. In terms of what is now affecting his living, is his mother's encroachment a more fundamental factor than his fear of trying himself out? Is the latter any less a cause of his present difficulties than the former? Characteristics engendered by certain circumstances may then themselves produce whole new sets of conditions. These developments (characteristics) are at once causes as well as effects rather than simply causes *or* effects. In terms of therapeutic operations, will learning that his mother took over for him be more of a factor in change than learning how to move in the face of fear (a problem with which people have to contend whether or not they had such a mother)? In shrinking from all kinds of normal challenges during his boyhood he has failed to develop certain essential powers. Is identifying and remedying the deficiencies in these powers less crucial to his present living than understanding the early protective experiences? Can we assume any longer the sufficiency and decisive value of interpreting the early experiences and their implications? In this light, it is difficult to assign standard priorities of significance and to define in advance which areas in a particular person are to receive the principal share of therapeutic effort. In each instance the clinician (even though he has already encountered recurrent themes in the lives of different people) has to make a fresh determination of what is significant for this particular person, what is he like, what concerns him, what has impact upon him, what kinds of characterization and activities make for change in him? In this approach any factor or system of substance warrants independent consideration until some other factor or system comes into focus.

The emphasis here is on finding what is what and this has many ramifications. If, for example, a person is passive, the first order of business is to know this characteristic thoroughly for what it is. As it stands, the word passive is more a concept than an experience of raw behavior. Qualities exist in the form of various behaviors and these behaviors are not quite encompassed by a term or concept. For a particular person passivity may mean (and what follows could not be known from the term itself): he does just enough in his work to keep it going; what he does isn't bad but it isn't good; he puts in his time yet he is subtly inactive; he follows the charted ways of working, rarely tries out his own ideas, is enlivened in the presence of forceful leadership; he drifts for long periods until circumstances demand something of him; if something difficult or troublesome arises he manages to be somewhere else; and so forth.

The assumption that a person really knows about his obvious characteristics is too readily made in psychotherapy. A person may appear to know himself, he may refer to himself as passive, but all too often this word is no more than a bit of sleight of hand that keeps him at a distance from himself. Many people prefer to use such terms to describe themselves rather than refer to behaviors, which contain the inescapable meanings. Other persons, immediately on hearing themselves characterized in a particular fashion, seem even more eager than the clinician-scientists to explore why he came to have this quality. In my opinion this is a form of defense, serving to dilute the impact of the characterization and to divert the work from a more profound appreciation of the quality. The clinician-scientist, ever poised to establish causes, may tend not to notice that people are interested in causes because it is easier to deal with them (however true they tend to rationalize one's condition) than it is to deepen one's experience of oneself. As a result, particularly in the early stages of the work, rather than attempt to account for a quality, it is preferable to go on to other situations in which the quality may be met at work. In my experience, establishing who and what the person is meets greater resistance than delving into causes. This is consistent with the great concern people evince about who and what they are. In fact, if one does not proceed according to set assumptions of what is significant, one finds out a great deal more about what actually affects people—what kind of language, what issues about themselves, whether, for instance, they are more troubled by discovering they are childishly demanding than by finding they have had some sexual impulses in relation to a parent.

Full appreciation of a quality is gained only after meeting its concrete manifestations in situation after situation. Furthermore this very procedure lays the groundwork for comprehending the shifting fields of cause and effect. Thus as we meet variations of passivity in the person mentioned earlier, we find that it occurs again and again in contexts where there is an older, presumably stronger person present, who, in effect, directs and steers. At this juncture we may dip into the past. We find in his family background a father who rather overwhelmed him by shows of force and power and who repeatedly hammered home the point that whatever the son needed could be gotten only through him. As new events develop reflecting his passivity, we notice that along with his passivity goes a very shrewd kind of calculation as to who and what will get him where. This constant calculation smothers his sense of what things really mean to him so that he is frequently confused or unknowing about what happened in specific situations. For a time then we may concentrate on helping the person sensitize himself to various aspects of himself, and although soon we may have to turn to another issue, we do so knowing that the issue we leave will swirl into the foreground on numerous subsequent occasions. Before long, in another event involving his passivity, we find that his essential sense of self, his feeling of resource, rests largely on the amount of money he has and the status this brings him socially. Because he actually has a great deal of money, patterns of affirmation (and their consequences) are readily, even passively, available to him. In any event, at this juncture we may attempt to define further what his identity consists of and how this structure affects his sense of adequacy and well-being. We go about this, not by getting his views of himself, but by being alert to the manifestations of this component of personality wherever it may appear in actual living. We may find in several discrete incidents that his money does something for him at the club, but that at a conference of colleagues on a matter of substance, he acts and feels like a mascot who looks on while the varsity plays the game. Exploring further his experiences at the conference, we come upon several cogent reactions that were neglected (unconscious) because their character was so alien to his general way of life that even the thought of giving them expression frightened him.

In the very process of learning who and what a person is, then, we come across factors that have consequences for one another and for his psychological status. These factors are simply distinctive qualities the very character of which directs us to related chains of consideration. At the same time these characteristics are of first order importance to the person himself, for he knows full well they as much measure as describe him.

This readiness to work with any aspect of personality that has the stature to define who and what the person is often frees the clinician from the confinements contingent upon the use of established concepts. If, for example, the function of interpretation is to enlarge awareness of significant considerations, then it can be readily seen that one's conception of the unconscious will affect the direction and content of interpretation. In this regard it has been rather generally assumed that the factors pushed out of awareness are those that tend to be repugnant to society and to the person in whom they exist. As a result we have tended to focus on factors regarded as unacceptable, such as aggression, sex, egocentricity, and so forth. However, many other aspects of the person, even "acceptable" aspects, may be kept out of awareness because those factors are not functional within the person's general mode of adaptation. Thus a passive person might not want to know his strengths, or a person who needs to please might want to avoid his individuality. As a consequence, such strengths and personal inclinations may be as deeply buried as any early memory and may require quite as much effort to draw out.

Consider the instance of a young woman who describes a typical evening spent with a particular young man, a writer. Their exchange is rather more a monologue than conversation, for this man talks constantly about himself, his life, his work, his views. The woman participates as a "good listener"—that is, she is attentive, nods admiringly here and there, and never considers changing the subject. As the evening ends, the man expresses his fast-growing appreciation of her appealing qualities. Only by means of a thorough-going elaboration of the experience, however, did it develop that she had registered vaguely a sense of this man's egocentricity and preciousness. Even more important were several penetrating but fleeting reactions she had during a discussion of some of his work. None of this comes into awareness or into play for it was bound to collide with her faith in pleasing. This kind of effort was often necessary for this person to make contact with dissociated potential not in itself repugnant to her.

*An Interview Illustrating*
*Some Aspects of Interpretation*

Once one escapes the ready "comprehension" afforded by concepts and correlations, the most difficult part of the interpretive process often turns out to be not so much seeing as bringing out what has to be seen. This is not to suggest, however, that interpretation or insight is secondary or without effect. The means of arriving at an insight are not to be confused with its effects. The fact that under particular conditions an insight may come readily does not mean it was already known, or even if known that it was used in living. Despite certain complications, degrees of accuracy and depth in knowing affect the resolution of psychological problems, as is the case in any kind of problem-solving.

Our concern at the moment, however, is less with the effects of self-understanding than with describing the process of arriving at an interpretation or insight. In this process the interaction between person and therapist can often be such that the experience of the session more or less speaks for itself, or at the very least, meanings fall easily into place. An example of this kind of interview follows. The excerpts given here were set down immediately after the session.

The person involved is a 21-year-old college senior who had been in therapy for about a year and a half. At the time she had considerable difficulty being close to anyone, tended to take a bright, let's-make-the-best-of-it attitude toward her problems, but often would lapse into feeling very low and forlorn for extended periods. Underneath her brisk intelligence, she was very uncertain of what things meant to her and was remarkably removed from what was actually going on in her. The interview begins with a brief survey of a weekend, in the course of which she refers gaily to a party at which she had been the object of considerable attention. After this introduction, we turn to particular aspects of the weekend.

P: Before going to the party, I spent a good part of the day with Peter, Jane's old boyfriend. You know they broke up, I think I told you. Jane isn't coming back to school anymore, but even before that—early this summer —they decided not to see each other anymore.

T: How did you happen to have a date with Peter?

P: Well, at the school dance—he was there. We talked a little. The next evening he called me and asked if we could get together. I told him I was coming into town on Saturday, though I had a party to go to at night. He said fine, to come in early and we'd spend the day, maybe go to a movie.

T: Well, how did it go?

P: I came in about 10, he wanted to go shopping. He needed some pants and also some shoes. I went along. We went down around the Village. Many of the stores were closed because of the holidays. Then he found a store, sort of an Army-Navy store but not quite, with lots of stock. He tried some trousers on, looked at some sweaters. He found some he liked. And bought it. In fact he put it right on. (*Pause*)

T: What did you do then?

P: Then he wanted some moccasins. He really didn't know where things were in the Village. He'd say well there's a store in that direction and then we'd wander around and not find it. But it didn't matter because it was a beautiful day and I liked walking around.

T: What did you do about the moccasins?

P: We finally found the store he had in mind. But it was closed. Across the street though there was another shoe store open and he went in there. He looked over some shoes and bought a pair.

T: Then?

P: We left the store and he asked if I'd like a beer. I said I was hungry and would like to eat something. He said he knew a little place a ways down. I said I wanted a sandwich, did it have that sort of thing. He said it has everything. I had an omelette there, he wasn't hungry, he just had a beer.

T: What did you talk about at lunch?

P: He told me about his interest in archeology. Somehow I thought he talked about things I had already known for quite a while. It was sort of familiar to me. I didn't take to it too much.

Then we left to go to see the movie "The Baker's Wife." But when we got there it had been on for an hour. So we went to see a movie I had seen a while ago, "The L-Shaped Room," a good movie.

At this point she shifted to another subject, remarking that she had to pick up some things she had left with an old boyfriend. Thus far there is not much in the material to suggest what the time spent with Peter meant to her; no phrase, tone, manner, or quality is registered or imparted by her in such a way as to give Peter existence. Inferences can be made about him from the sequence of events, but very little is available through the medium of direct experience. Indeed in the reconstructed material up to this point, Peter comes through a little more palpably than he did in the interview itself. Conceivably one could have interpreted to her at this juncture the probability that she does not know what Peter means to her, that she goes along in brisk superficiality, losing the depths of her reactions, and is thus left unknowing about what is happening to her. In this instance, however, the interpretation was deferred in the expectation that opening up the experience further would make for a profounder appreciation of the problem. For this reason the therapist brought the person back to the day spent with Peter.

T: I have the feeling there is more to go through in the time you spent with Peter. Let's see, when did you meet with him?

P: Oh we met early. About 10. At the railroad station. He's staying at a friend's just before going back to college.

T:   What does Peter look like?

P:   Oh he's kind of tall. Though as you know he seems just about average to me. What with my father being 6'5" someone who is 6' seems just about average. Solid but not heavy. Not bad looking.

T.   What did he look like when you met him that day?

P:   It was sort of funny. He looked sort of shabby. He was wearing a beat up pair of corduroy pants. He hadn't shaven. And his moccasins were too small for him, so the backs had been stepped on so much they looked like a bedroom slipper.

T:   What did he have to say when you met?

P:   Well he said he needed some clothes. Would I like to come shopping with him. I said fine. He didn't know where things were so we did a lot of walking. Then we found that clothing store.

T:   And can we go over that again?

P:   Well he looked at sweaters and trousers. He didn't ask me for my opinion of things. He didn't seem to want anybody else's reaction. He just kept looking over things and trying them on.

T:   What did you do in the meantime?

P:   I sort of looked at people in the store. And made some small talk with the owner. Sometimes I said I like this or that, a sweater, for instance. I don't know what he had me along for, he didn't seem to want the feminine reaction. Once we talked about the price of a sweater— that it seemed a good buy for the money.

T:   Then what?

P:   We went looking for the moccasins, which took quite a bit of wandering about. After we were through with this was when he asked me if I wanted a beer.

T:   About what time was this?

P:   It was about 2 o'clock. I said I had eaten at about 8 and was hungry. He had eaten about 10. I said I wanted to go to a place that had some food like sandwiches. He said he knew a little place nearby, he had had a beer there. It turned out they didn't have sandwiches so I had an omelette.

T:   Can we go over again what you talked about?

P:   As I said, it was about his new interest in archeology. He was talking about some diggings, and what some of the things found revealed about the society. (*Apparently he went on about this at some length.*) It was not of that much interest to me because this work is fairly familiar to me. (*She has a major in archeology.*)

T:   I suspect he didn't look at you very much when he talked.

P:   How did you know that? It happens to be true.

T:   I know it because somewhere you know it but you go on in a way which makes it very hard for you to know it.

It took no great leap, given this man's unrelatedness, to assume that he did not notice her lack of interest and probably did not even look at her very much. We then went into other aspects of the day that ostensibly had already been covered. With each succeeding round the material was enlarged from a bare report of events to an account that by its very nature moved both person and therapist. For example, it developed that this young man had not at any time asked her whether she had had enough of shopping or whether she was hungry. Because they had met at 10:00 and he had known she had been traveling for about an hour, he had some basis for assuming that she had had breakfast early. When he did bring up the question of food or drink, it was in terms of something he wanted at the moment—namely, a beer.

As this material developed the therapist asked whether she had known, before she looked into her day with Peter, how she felt about seeing him again. Her answer was that if he had called she probably would have gone out with him again. Now, however, she was a little taken aback by the many reservations she found in herself and doubted that she would care to spend another day like this. Along the line, the therapist noted how difficult it was for her to give a direct sense of Peter, which made it evident that her own experience was not available to her. In this context she was asked to try to imitate Peter's voice or manner, which she found almost impossible to do. Reality itself then demonstrated how she short-circuits experience and how this leaves her without direction or confidence. Much, of course, remained to be absorbed about this issue, which in the very process of being defined raised many questions for future work. In this session, however, the issue is defined not in the form of a thought, but rather emerges from experience and thus becomes an experience. At the same time the session itself is an exercise that she very much needs to repeat in coming to herself.

### Summary with Proviso

The keystone of interpretation is experience, not a system of findings or concepts. Experience develops in the flow of life, in events and situations rather than in thoughts or ideas. Interpretation involves the apprehension of the nature and character of another person by means of participating in this person's life experiences. As the person in therapy goes through the redintegration of events of his life, new events are created in therapy, the mutual experience of which becomes the source of organismic rather than intellectual understanding. These new events may, of course, be partially shaped by experientially rooted communications (interpretations) by the therapist. His expertness, however, lies not so much in his capacity to formulate interpretations as in his ability to generate events. In this view therapy involves a shuttling back and forth between experiences and the brief contemplation of these experiences. Interpretation in the narrow sense, and for that matter meanings of any sort, are useful only insofar as they can be experienced by the person to whom they are offered. If the interpretation touches what the person is going through, whether in or out of awareness, it can be deeply recognizable, for the chemistry of the experience is still warm and the data of verification are right at hand.

Not all aspects of a person's functioning, however, necessarily reflect the experience the person is having. Indeed some activities obscure the experience. Consequently it is very important in therapy to develop an ear for the essential experience. At any one time a person may have several activities going on, among which there is usually one that vitally involves his capacities and feelings. This latter is the real thing that he is going through, the experience that is actually affecting him.

Consider the example of a woman who, in talking about her relationship to her husband, acknowledges a long history of having criticized him chiefly because of her own irrational needs. She goes on to say that, nevertheless, he actually has many qualities that are hard to live with. He often upbraids her in public; he stands on his position in social situations; he seeks sinecures in his work; he comes home and spends the evening watching television; the evening is punctuated by fits of temper; and so forth. As one hears this bill of particulars, however, what comes through is that this person is less involved with what she is saying than with how she is saying it. One senses that in her mind's eye she is impressed with the impassioned note in her voice, with the toss of her head, with the eloquence of her language. She is not coming to grips with the actual problem of living with her husband; rather she is taken up with painting a momentarily reassuring portrait of the high-flying possibilities of her personality. As it happens, this is for her a characteristic mode of functioning; she is often deflected from dealing with real problems by an interior process of ego-building. Very little would come of trying to discuss her husband, for this is not her focus but is only a pretext for an experience in quite a different realm. The problem of identifying the main experience is often difficult, but failure to do so accounts in part for how it is that apparently accurate interpretations fail to take. Although the interpretation may be unerringly related to certain material developed by the person, that material may not actually be in the stream of the central experience. When content and experience are one, then the content can be responded to without reservation.

## The Problem of Artificiality

Interpretation as a function of experience is significantly affected by the unavoidable artificiality of therapy. Artificiality in therapy is a consequence of the necessary restrictions placed upon the degree of involvement between person and therapist. Events in therapy cannot take their natural course and as a result important qualities of both person and therapist may not be brought into play. Some of the so-called love or admiration transferences, for instance, would not last long were the two people actually living together. Although the therapeutic arrangement protects both people from these and other vulnerabilities and particularly keeps the therapist's needs from blurring his vision, carried too far it renders the experience academic. The absence of lifelike interaction is the source of artificiality in therapy. On the other hand therapy can be more or less lifelike, depending on whether its emphasis is on events or on words and ideas.

An incident that illustrates these issues concerns a particular person who had been seen in therapy for some time. At the very beginning of one hour she asked the therapist whether she could borrow a certain book he had in the office. Without thinking he said yes, but even as he did he realized that the request had a disturbing effect. He then asked how she happened to decide to borrow this book. She answered that she had had difficulty in getting this book from the library and had recalled she had seen the book in his office. She went on to say that usually she does not like to borrow books, but she thought he would not mind. When did it occur to her to borrow the book? Out in the waiting room just before the hour began. What was going through her mind out there? Sitting outside she was thinking that the therapist was seeing a particular woman that she had noticed often passing through the waiting room. This had led her to wonder what he was like with other people who came to see him, whether he ever became involved with them socially or even lent a book to someone now and then. With further development a familiar theme emerged—namely, her insistent wish to be the favorite, the one most important and closest to the elder in a situation. As this became clear to the person, she said, in effect, this is all very much so, certainly I have to turn this over in my mind; and now will you lend me the book? The request repeated under these circumstances led the therapist to answer that he would rather not. Thereupon she became angry and reproachful, a great deal more so than could be accounted for by any social delicacy in the occurrence. Thus, the situation, organized by maladaptive needs (itself an event), brought a negative action from the therapist rather than an analysis. This precipitated another event that made meaningful in experience the extent to which the person follows her insistent aims and is paying only lip-service to the possibility of change.

Some varieties of acting out create events and thus provide a basis for knowing. A student therapist describes a session with a thirteen-year-old girl who is rather vague and subtly helpless. On this occasion the girl had come alone to the clinic by subway. During the session she speaks at some length about how frightening she had found the experience. After the session the therapist walks with her to the station, gives her detailed directions, and indicates that she can ask the conductor for help if she needs any. Just before the train door closes, the therapist points to the conductor and says, "And that is the conductor." Thereupon he is surprised to notice that the girl gives him a baleful glance. The incident seems to be as much a product of the therapist's personality as the girl's; how-

ever, he is living (creating) his experience of the girl—
that is, in pointing out the conductor as if she were a five-
year-old. Were the sense of his behavior to rise to awareness, it would constitute an appreciation of the girl in
depth. This mode results in another order of knowing,
comparable to touching rather than only seeing velvet.

This incident is a little more on the side of unconscious
acting out, but still it illustrates the possibilities for understanding available in events. The difficulty is not so much
the acting out as the degree of the therapist's awareness
of himself in the situation. This approach can be useful
if it begins with some glimmer on the therapist's part that
he is starting some event to see what it brings. As long as
the involvement is not wild or in poor judgment, such developments extend the range and reality of therapeutic
experience. The procedure must be controlled, but it must
allow enough freedom for an alternation between letting
things happen and absorbing the significance of these hap-
penings.

## Style of Interpretation

In regard to how to interpret—that is, the means and
manner of communicating with the person—there is relatively little to say. If one works in the mode described
here, one probably will use a form and language natural
to one's individuality. It is not likely to be a conceptual
language; fussiness is apt to be referred to as fussiness
rather than as compulsiveness. It will thus tend to have
the psychological precision of the vernacular rather than
the pseudo-precision of technical parlance.

There are doubtless ways of refining one's capacity for communication, but it would be a mistake to confuse effectiveness with style. Devices, verbal or otherwise, have a dismal record of performance in psychotherapy. Style, of course, may lend certain meaningful touches to the work. Certainly, for example, a particular quality may be better illuminated by means of an apt parable than by a direct description of the quality. If one can and likes to make a point in the Hassidic or Zen-Buddhist manner or even as a Western raconteur, so much the better. In this connection I happen to think that a language rich in imagery reinstates experience. I would therefore prefer a statement such as, "So much of the time you look like a lost little waif," over "You are always asking for attention." Yet I would not be able strenuously to maintain that the former is more effective, because the latter stated genuinely and simply is a perfectly meaningful reaction.

Refinements may delight and even improve communication by degrees; nevertheless, the firmest foundation of communication is the natural, unselfconscious expression of one's experience. This is not the same as "spontaneously" saying any thing that comes to mind, which usually is a shallow kind of communication. Faculties of sense, discrimination, and judgment are integral aspects of effective communication and do not impair spontaneity unless misused.

Style notwithstanding, a little clumsy fumbling for perceptions is frequently an indispensable way of bringing them to light. Experience does not always speak in a loud and clear voice. Sometimes it is a delicate, not particularly logical whisper at the edge of one's mind. Despite its indistinctness, it may nevertheless give off the sense that grasping it will make for some unpleasant moments in the course of therapy. For such reasons these apprehensions may readily be passed over. Yet many perceptions in life and in therapy begin in just this slight and nebulous fashion. Moving toward and exploring these fragile "thoughts" is often a prelude to important and solid conclusions. On the hunch that such a will-o'-the-wisp may amount to something, one reaches for it, trying, even clumsily, to express it or to raise a question that may bear on it or even to remark that one is left with a vague sense of this or that but cannot quite carry it farther. Any of these reactions may initiate an interaction that leads to a clarification of the perception. Even so inelegant a procedure can eventuate in powerful apprehensions.

Occasionally, perhaps rarely, there is a basis for believing that some force or quality exists in a person, but one cannot seem to sense it directly. Such a situation is of interest because it may reflect a possible breakdown of the method and thus may help define the limits of experience as a means for knowing another person. An event of this kind does not necessarily demonstrate deficiencies in the method, however, for it may be that not enough is known about how to bring out certain aspects of people, or perhaps that certain operating assumptions have the effect of obscuring experience.

Interpretation, despite expertness and knowledgeability on the part of the therapist, is ultimately a matter of personal apprehension. Fromm, in fact, has suggested in clinical seminars that interpretation be considered simply the therapist's response or reaction. This view, of course, has implications for "style." In particular it renders inappropriate the style associated with authority, even legitimate authority, which in other fields derives from a body of verified knowledge. The psychotherapist is not in a position *to instruct* the person on the authoritative meaning of his "illness." This situation has advantages for both parties. The person quickly learns that what is really available to him are the *reactions* of a trained and experienced individual and that it is up to him to determine what these reactions mean to him. Such a relationship thus places the person in the center of the work; it underlines the necessity for sifting and weighing what is offered and even for leading the search. The therapist, on the other hand, is not constrained to adopt the posture of authority; he does not have to stand on his view or theory as representing the final word on human nature. This attitude will save him from painful contortions as he discovers that in any case there is no such final word. Thus collaboration is improved even as mystique is reduced.

## Limits of Interpretation

The limits of interpretation very nearly coincide with the limits of insight in effecting change. Acknowledged but still inadequately understood are a number of factors affecting movement in therapy which are not encompassed by the concept of insight or its corollary, resistance. Among these are temperamental factors; the effect of certain aspects of the environment (specific interpersonal relationships); nonconceptual therapeutic experiences that sometimes facilitate a breakthrough to depths of feeling; germinal encounters in therapy and elsewhere with possibilities of living; and learning to make effective use of self (an enterprise having more to do with discernment, experimentation, and sagacity than with insight into "psychodynamics").

Reliance on the associated concepts of insight and resistance has tended to conceal for too long our lack of knowledge about processes of change. We may often go over material again and again with all the means at our disposal but not enough seems to come of it. Under these circumstances the analyst is very likely to resort to resistance as an explanation. Yet on many occasions the stalemate may define the limits of our knowledge rather than resistance.

Suppose, for instance, we are working with a markedly egocentric person. Assume that the person has learned a good deal in therapy about the existence, effects, and origins of this characteristic. In some people this insight releases energies that make for change and growth. For many other persons the spark flares for a moment, perhaps even again and again, but is not sustained. As this person becomes aware of her egocentric quality, she may try to do something about it. It may very well occur to her, for example, that unselfishness is the opposite of self-involvement. This may then be followed by attempts at behaving unselfishly, usually in terms of some socially agreed upon conception of unselfishness. Such a course often ends in defeat because outward reform is substituted for a change of heart; yet many follow this course not knowing what else to do.

Current knowledge does not offer much information about the psychological processes that regulate such an interior change. Interpretation affording psychodynamic insight is not the only approach to this particular problem;

in fact it is only grossly attuned to the problem. As one alternative the problem can be seen in these terms: Psychologically, the opposite of egocentricity is not unselfishness but rather openness and responsiveness. A person cannot react to that which he does not take in. The improvement of such a condition requires activities in therapy that go beyond the familiar work of interpretation and insight.

As an illustration consider a clinical incident involving the egocentric person mentioned above. One afternoon this person is reviewing with her instructor a paper she had written on Spanish literature. It happens that this person is much concerned with approval and with establishing a special place with such figures as teachers. As the paper is discussed what runs through her mind, more or less unconsciously, is how does he react to me, how exactly does he like to have things done, what will it take to get him to like me and be on my side. This is important therapeutic material but other considerations warrant equal attention. Characteristically preoccupied with herself and with establishing a particular interpersonal arrangement, she can hardly concentrate, think, or express herself in relation to the subject itself. At best she is using her wits and intelligence to find what will go over. In a certain sense she is being irrelevant. Not unexpectedly the report is organized about one or two ideas much in vogue these days and therefore rather likely to be accepted. However, it is lacking in intimacy, understanding and individuality, which is to say it is lacking in mind.

All of this has a great deal to do with egocentricity. Although she gets by, she does not know her subject well and senses that her mind is not of much use to her in dealing with the real problems she meets in life. Apart from some shrewdness in working out benevolent relationships, her functioning in relation to issues of substance can only leave her feeling weak and ineffectual. With so little power being generated, is there an alternative to continuing to be worried about herself? Does not this state of affairs require that she go on trying to get other persons to be concerned with her as well? Once caught on this track she gets very little practice in being responsive to problems, objects, or people outside herself. In short she is far too ineffectual, inexperienced, and undernourished to have anything left for anyone else.

In therapy the person can be brought into contact with these issues, can experiment with attention, concentration, and involvement and with finding her own reactions. By their very nature these activities differ from egocentricity, so that without wrestling directly with the problem, they may have effects on this trait.

Similar difficulties may be found to be affecting other functions, such as the capacity for feeling. Another person, for instance, tends to deal with situations that he does not handle very well with the following verbal reverie: "Yet I know I mean well. I know I do. These things happen despite my best efforts." Such words often bring tears to his eyes. This is probably a form of sentimentality. Such a person is potentially capable of genuine feeling, but the rub here is that sentimentality displaces feeling with thought. Sentimentality, inherently self-justifying and reassuring to the ego, dilutes affect by removing it from its natural locus, rendering it shallow and less related. This mode of functioning can be affected in various ways. The person can, for example, sensitize himself to the degree of self-consciousness in his responses and try to alter the typical course of such functioning by turning from self-oriented reveries to his immediate reality. Specific efforts can be made to free feeling from such encumbrances.

These examples emphasize that therapy cannot rest so heavily on interpretation and insight. The objective of the person knowing himself must in any event be broadened beyond the usual variety of psychodynamic self-knowledge. The person needs to know not only the mainsprings of his behavior, his qualities as a person, but he has to become in his own way a student of human nature. He has to know what conditions of living and functioning induce in him a state of well-being. This state, as Fromm has made clear, provides a criterion against which to gauge the value of one's experiments and efforts.[6] He has to learn something about the generation and decay of various powers and faculties and how to come to awareness about himself. No one can define for him the reaches of his individuality, but he needs to learn that there are ways of getting there and that in fact only he may be able to find these ways.

6. A view expressed by Fromm in clinical seminars held in Mexico during the summer of 1957.

# *Six*

# RESISTANCE

*RESISTANCE* is an unremitting and yet elusive problem in psychotherapy. Broadly, resistance refers to a familiar but disconcerting phenomenon, namely, that people do not change readily, even when they want to. This observation will not come as a surprise to anyone moderately in touch with himself or his fellow man. Continuous exposure on the part of psychotherapists to this problem has transformed causual appreciation into a grave regard for the size of the obstacles that block the path of change.

*Concepts of Resistance*

It is not easy to set down a straightforward definition of resistance. Freud regarded resistance as any means that the patient used to interfere with the course of treatment,[1] all of which he saw rooted dynamically in the "repulsion from unconscious ideas."[2] Actually the meaning of the concept was amplified by the way it was applied in practice. In the early stages of psychoanalytic therapy the concept was related to the conviction that the cause and cure of neurosis had been determined. The cause was taken to be certain irregular experiences involving the libido; the method of cure involved recovering these experiences, seeing into their significance, and thus freeing the libido. In this context resistance referred to anything that got in the way of developing insight into the infantile libidinal origins of neurosis. Thus it was said to be at work when a person did not or could not follow the fundamental rule of free association, when he was unable to recall infantile memories, when he openly or subtly did not accept the therapist's interpretations, when he came late, or when he lived out the infantile libidinal attachments with the therapist (transference resistance) and thereby evaded recollection of early events. At first, then, resistance was seen as manifesting itself in limited behaviors designed to keep these ultimate factors in the dark. The reluctance to come to grips with these issues was assumed to derive from the unpleasant, unacceptable, and even frightening elements

1. Sigmund Freud, *A General Introduction to Psychoanalysis* (New York: Liveright, 1935), pp. 253–259.
2. Freud, *Collected Papers*, IV, p. 27.

inherent in early libidinal development (Oedipus Complex, castration fears, and so forth).

A major stride forward was taken by Wilhelm Reich, who vastly extended the concept and at the same time accepted in essence the above scheme of thought.[3] He advanced the position of his day by noting that the problem of resistance goes beyond the use of temporary devices to evade awareness. People, he observed, have more or less permanent modes of behaving (character traits) that present firmly consolidated obstacles to the development of insight. Thus a person with anal character traits, stubborn and obstructive, would tend to hold back material or would cooperate only grudgingly in the procedures of the analysis. Reich, however, did not grant character itself a fundamental adaptive significance. He did not see character as representing a person's functional solution to living and as therefore itself the ultimate issue of psychotherapy. Though richly sensitive to qualities of character, in the end he regarded character as a series of fixed defenses that serve to cloud the early roots of neurosis. In his scheme, once the person learned about the existence and function of these traits, the person could then go on with the indispensable work of recovering the infantile amnesias. Although Reich chose to consider the libido as the factor of ultimate significance, his work on character started a chain of developments still in process today.

Any concept both illuminates and channels the mind. By relating resistance so immediately to the unpleasantness of looking into the libidinal roots of neurosis, the early

3. Wilhelm Reich, *Character Analysis* (New York: Orgone Institute Press, 1949).

analysts emphasized the element of choice in the concept. Consciously or otherwise, resistance involved the choice of avoidance. It lent the concept the connotation of willed opposition to facing the facts about oneself and thus made of resistance a rather specific form of motivation. Certainly this describes an important variety of resistance as it is met in life and in therapy. Apart from its applicability, the early analysts would have been inclined to stress this particular aspect of the concept, for in the authoritarian spirit of the European physician-patient relationship, failure to accept interpretations or even to get better, would have been put down to willful resistance.

Precisely because the concept, narrowly defined, had so much meaning, it was difficult to see the problem as larger than a specific kind of motivation. Whereas resistance is often nothing more than unwillingness to face some disagreeable facts; frequently this unwillingness is indicative of deeper conditions. Some persons function in such a way that they cannot hear the truth; some hear it but do not know what to do with it; some do not have the resources to bear the truth; and some are not helped by knowing the truth because the circumstances of their lives are insuperable.

Disengaged from the objective of insight and viewed in the perspective of general personality change, the concept of resistance takes on new dimensions. In this perspective it becomes difficult to maintain a narrow definition of resistance. What appears as unwillingness to see oneself realistically, sometimes only conceals an inescapable dilemma. Many aspects of personality that obstruct therapy are not encompassed by the narrow definition of resistance. Suppose, for example, a person tends to come late to therapy or is very passive in the therapeutic work. Such behavior could of course reflect resistance. If, however, this person tends to be late or passive in most things he does, are we then dealing with resistance or character? Although such behavior certainly obstructs therapy, it can hardly be conceived that its major function is to serve this end. Behavior of this sort does not come into existence in order to evade knowing oneself, though inadvertently it may have this effect. Rather it simply represents how the person typically goes about things in his life.

Consider the implications for therapy and resistance of a vivacious, talkative woman, who characteristically has little sense of the reality and finality of life. This quality is best exemplified in a dream she reports during one session: She is careering along in a car. Although she is supposed to be the driver, she only now and then manages to get her hand on the wheel. In the car she is busy, sometimes frantically trying to get the children to stay in their place, sometimes she is fussing in the back seat, occasionally out of the corner of her eye she sees traffic and buildings streaming by. Throughout she feels the car is going faster than it ought to be and she might get a ticket. She hopes nothing will happen. By this time she is getting close to where she is to meet her husband. She thinks even if she does get a ticket, perhaps her husband will be able to talk the policeman out of it.

In the dream she is busy either with frantic fussing or is preoccupied with minor legalities at a time when her life and the lives of others are at stake. In the absence of contact with the real situation, no sense of urgency or danger is generated. The diffusion of reality places serious limits on what she can do in therapy, but the same is true in many other areas of her life. Situations and problems in her life are not lived with and worked through. Difficulties may be identified and deplored, but no sooner is this done then she loses herself in glowing fantasies about alternatives. There is no question but that this characterological problem obstructs the resolution of many issues, but can this be categorized as resistance? If this problem is disposed of as resistance—that is, as a secondary phenomenon—then it is likely not to receive the amount of direct therapeutic work needed to deepen the person's sense of reality.

One of the paradoxes of therapy, often seen in relation to resistance, is illustrated in the above situation. Not infrequently the very trait that broadly obstructs change also obstructs its own alteration. The mode that blurs reality also blurs the reality of the mode itself. (Also in many instances such a trait may for various reasons be dearly valued by the person himself.) For such reasons, therapy often seems to be in the position of asking people to lift themselves by their own bootstraps. The volitional aspect of the human being is such that this is actually possible to some degree. Indeed will is one of the strongest forces we can call on in therapy, but mainly for short hauls and in relation to immediate and limited objectives. Without this capacity the person would be a machine, utterly subject to external control; therapy as we know it would not be possible. Each time we identify resistance we are in effect asking the person to mobilize his resources and to bring them to bear on his problems. This can and must be done in therapy many times and in different ways, but experience demonstrates that such methods are not equal to the task of sustaining movement in therapy.

The following material illustrates this point, as well as certain other issues that we have been discussing in relation to resistance. The person concerned, Mr. K, is a thirty-five-year-old, free-lance industrial designer, married, with a two-year-old son and his wife six-months pregnant, who comes into therapy with a persistent fear that some nameless injury or disease will befall him. With his earnings irregular and just enough to subsist on, and gnawed by the question of whether there will be enough money to cover the arrival of the baby, it develops that his business is so arranged as to leave him in an exceedingly vulnerable position. Eighty-five per cent of his work is referred by a single agent-middleman, who alternately scolds or praises Mr. K and often requires special revisions without additional payment. The agent knows only too well that as Mr. K's major source of income, he more or less holds him in thrall. Despite his vulnerability, Mr. K for several years now has made no effort to diversify the sources of his income. During a particular session it becomes amply clear that this situation must be the source of considerable anxiety for Mr. K and that his being in such a predicament must define him in significant ways. After the session he rings for the elevator and finds these words coming out of his mouth, "That's not going to change me!" He could not have been more correct, for when he comes in next time, he can barely remember what had gone on in the previous session. All he recalls is that we had talked about something that vaguely concerned his work.

The extent of resistance is only too evident; the question is how to deal with it. Typically such resistance is interpreted, which was done in this instance, but with little observable effect, even over a period of time. The reluctance to absorb anything about himself is equally clear in other areas. As therapy goes on it becomes apparent that he is deeply bound to his mother and that in many ways he lives the life of a sheltered youngster. One of his profoundest unconscious convictions is that he will not be able to survive without her. In fact he has a dream in which he finds a room in his present apartment he did not know was there. When he opens the door he is astonished to find his mother is living in this room. It is not a matter of chance then, that his economic survival depends upon one person.

Although such meanings are encountered repeatedly in incident and dream, he does not really absorb them. Resistance prevails. Gradually, however, it becomes clear that he has no alternative but to keep these issues vaguely apprehended, for as things stand he simply does not have the wherewithal to alter his life. The way he is presently functioning provides practically no leverage for changing himself or his life. In regard to work, for example, it develops that his designs have many flaws even to the nonexpert eye. Defects are left uncorrected, corners are cut, the finish is unprofessional, only rarely does he let himself reach for a daring effect, and so on. The area of interpersonal relations is equally unnourishing. In his relationships he stands on his precociousness, displaying his promise, seeking to please, but often failing to act cogently or effectively. Without basic competence, he understands instinctively that facing the nature of his business arrangements or of his relationship to his mother is intolerable and will only injure further an already lacerated sense of self-esteem.

Instead of continuing along these lines, "working through" that is, we turn instead to a concrete psychological study of how he works. We find, for example, that he knows very well when he makes an error, but he is inclined to let it pass and see whether it will get by. In the process he neglects his own sensibilities and conceptions in favor of standards set by someone else. Rarely does he feel that the work produced is his own. At this point we concentrate on his making use of what he observes about his work, on finding and applying his own standards, on reaching for and developing rudimentary ideas. Even to the nonexpert eye there is a steady improvement in the caliber of his work. This is followed by a crisis, which lasts about two or three months, concerning whether he can now bring himself to test his "new" powers by showing his work to other clients, which among other things might help break the hold of his agent. During these months it becomes apparent he is desperately afraid of making this move. We agree, however, that he is roughly ready for this step, that to discuss anything else is only a diversion or a postponement, and that we simply have to live continuously with the issue: Either he moves in the face of fear or he does not. Finally he makes the leap. His work interests other clients, and the demand for his work increases markedly. (Work comparable to this is being carried on in other areas, such as his interpersonal relationships.) In a parallel development, he begins to take in a great deal more about his relationship to his mother. Dreams appear in which involvement with his mother leads to his almost missing the boat; action follows in which, for example, he protects his marriage from intrusions by the mother.

Resistance then, even when expressed in classic form, is not necessarily a problem in itself. Inadequacy in work, for instance, is unlikely to yield to interpretations about psychodynamics and resistance. The apprehension of the more usual psychodynamics may be facilitated or even made possible, not by the interpretation of resistance, but rather by the clinical analysis of the inadequacy itself and by the implementation of this analysis in action.

## Conditions Of Resistance

The first condition of resistance, in my opinion, is the tenacity of character itself. As a body of long-standing traits, habits, canalizations, conditionings, character is a deeply etched structure. Psychology indeed appears to have its own modest law of inertia; people maintain a staunch and unvarying rate of motion and direction unless this arrangement is disrupted by some other force. *Character becomes second nature* and no one expects "nature" to be easily undone. In accenting this property of character, I am not implying immutability or inherency; I am simply emphasizing its phenomenological durability. Appreciation of the sources of drag in psychotherapy may improve the chances of responding to inertia relevantly. In dealing with the fixity of character, methods have to be related to such issues as faith, ingrained sets, indoctrination, conditioning, and general integration. Many of the current methods of psychotherapy bear on these issues, but often inexplicitly and without intention. The unexpected response of the therapist to a characteristic that normally elicits a different response is in itself a deconditioning procedure— one, however, that occurs in a humanizing context. The view that regards character as having first-order rather than secondary significance leads to extended work with specific traits, quite apart from conventional psychodynamics. The problem of resistance centers about character and does not yield to what at times becomes incantations about motivation, choice, or existence. This tenacity is likely to be underestimated because so much of how one lives can be made to seem a matter of belief, judgment, and taste. Such professions of choice make it appear that the person is living exactly the life he has designed for himself.

It is not an overstatement to suggest that the requirements of the work in everyday therapy are comparable to asking a devout and orthodox person to undertake of his own volition a radical examination of the worth and utility of his religion. The venture is to be undertaken, furthermore, only if the person commits himself in advance to change whatever he finds wanting, no matter where the chips may fall. The recoil of the orthodox would be immediately visible. By contrast, in therapy the person does not come teeth-set to defend his outlook. Observing one side of certain ambivalences the ever-hopeful, therapist may even be persuaded that the person's desire to change will carry the day. The therapist would be in for less disillusionment, however, if in almost every instance he assumed the power of the forces opposed to change to be of the order met when the orthodox are asked to renovate their temples.

"Orthodoxy" for each person is his particular answer to life, which often can be condensed into a relatively simple theme. "I am safe as long as I am led by father." "If I achieve every social propriety and success I'll be loved." "I always do the good and the right so I'm invulnerable." "A rule can be found for every situation in life if only one looks hard enough." There are, of course, people who build on a relatively constructive theme—love, let us say, rather than power—which is maintained with no less tenacity than the former type.

Themes are rarely asserted directly; if anything one hears the opposite. One is told, for example, "I like to do things for myself." In time, however, one finds this statement has a secret and invariable inclusion: "But I won't because I want to believe you have the power to do it for me." The quality of tenacity (resistance) often takes this silent and parenthetical form. For these reasons long periods of exposure to the person are required to come upon the negation of what is expressed. A theme of this sort is the hardy foundation of a philosophy of life that has an elaborate scaffolding; yet each story that rises is in many respects a variation of the central design.

Tenacity of character is compounded of many considerations. Character infuses nature in childhood when every fiber is soft and impressionable. Childhood furthermore is a period of relative powerlessness, a significant condition which establishes the almightiness of parents. It is at this time, when innocence, love, and faith make for the greatest receptiveness, or when disapproval and anger are experienced probably as a threat to survival, that the major teachings and indoctrinations are implanted. Whether the circumstances of childhood are negative or positive, forces exist that tend to stamp in and brace traits of character. To have ways of living is a matter of adaptive necessity. Constant usage digs deep furrows on nature—which alone would suggest that alteration would require considerable time and effort. As time goes on, character is usually perpetuated by the selection of people to live with who make one's ways seem valid and necessary. Furthermore in the nature of man there is a deep need for stability and order. This need is served as characterological solutions lend a structure to living, which renders precious the solutions per se. Whatever integration we achieve is hard won, for people neither contemplate further change with ease nor do they relish the prospect of reverting to an earlier level of functioning. Regression notwithstanding, very few people yearn to be children again, not because it was necessarily an unhappy time but because it is understood to be a period of latency and therefore relative powerlessness. The arduousness of development has the effect of having both the past and the future press in to maintain the present.

Certain traits of character need especially to be mentioned for the contribution they make to inertia. Foremost among these is the disposition to talk thought rather than express experience. This mode of functioning is very common and is perhaps the most efficient of the various "defenses." Many people have learned to tell about what they "think" happened, rather than simply what happened. Thoughts generated in this way rarely penetrate the dynamisms of affect, with the result that nothing moves. Because thought and words can be used to construct meanings, people can create a "reality" of their own and often persuade others of it. Thoughts are much more malleable than reality; consequently they can be shaped to suit psychological convenience. People learn with great subtlety to leave out the rub of reality, which in turn takes the earth out of reactions. Another such significant trait I will refer to as insincerity for want of a better term. Some people have for so long played loose with what they really mean that they are actually at a loss to know what really matters to them. Their desire or capacity to find what is authentic in a heartfelt way has somehow gone astray. In such instances the work seems to slide and glide, nothing takes firmly. Inertia is also materially affected by the degree to which the person cares about himself. Certain people who look like going concerns have had hope so severely battered that unconsciously they care very little about what happens to them. One more quality of importance is an incapacity for sustained effort. Traits of the type just listed will defeat movement unless their priority is appreciated and they are quickly and steadily taken on in the work.

Another series of considerations bearing on inertia are rather more existential than characterological in shading. The psychological tendency to avoid doubt, uncertainty, and unease is as profound in its own right as the biological tendency to avoid pain. On all sides we are presented with opportunities for keeping clear of uncertainty—ideologies, fervent religious answers, black and white positions. These systems are designed not only to still the doubts of other persons but those of the propagators as well. The more people who subscribe to the system, the righter it seems. Doubt and question in some moderate degree is a necessary condition for psychological growth. The alternative is to leap into quick answers that settle only inadequately the persistent perplexities of life.

Associated with this factor but sufficiently separate to be considered independently is the fear of something new, different, or unknown. This is all the greater when there is something about the new that draws one but is difficult to achieve. It is not only a matter of unsettling a workable order. Even if things are quite unsatisfactory, there is an explicit fear of trying something new to put in its place.

The distant person, though distressed about this very quality, is all at once annoyed, threatened, and drawn to a person in whom he sees a capacity for responsiveness and closeness. Again it is a fear that works swiftly and silently, one not readily experienced, though it does on occasion give clear signs of itself. During one session, for example, a person notices a quality in his analyst that evokes appreciation and respect. In the course of the day he reflects on it now and then. That night just before he falls asleep it flashes into his mind that the analyst has murdered his wife, a thought which irrationally demolishes the analyst and what he stands for. (A month or so before this incident this analyst's wife actually had died.) In relation to new challenges there are often dreams of having to leap from a high place or navigate in turbulent rapids. One day the industrial designer described earlier interrupts the usual course of his procrastination and completes a piece of work quite to his own satisfaction. That night he has a dream in which he toys with the idea of returning to a previous analyst, an act that would run counter to his conscious inclinations.

Both Sullivan and Fromm direct attention to yet another source of resistance—that is, the fear that change may result in isolation. Sullivan notes that changes in behavior may call forth disapproval from those having a stake in the person staying the same. Fromm refers to the phenomenon as an explicit fear of ostracism. Surely one's sense of validity and belonging depends in some degree on whether one is acceptable or unacceptable to one's group. I suspect, however, that the more one's security is essentially interpersonal rather than individual (not that one can exclude the other), the more resistance one would encounter in the effort to know oneself. Loosely connected to social arrangements, but not to be underestimated out of familiarity, is the factor of secondary gain. This simply means that when maladaptive ways work after a fashion, the use of these ways tends to be perpetuated.

Lastly, untried and inexperienced persons tend in particular to maintain familiar directions, for it is yet to be demonstrated to them that certain of their ways produce an unhappiness all their own. These insufficiencies have to be brought home over a period of time, inadvertently or otherwise, by figures and events in the person's life. Few people volunteer to change; life has to demand it of them. For these reasons therapy with adolescents, for example, is especially difficult. A variant of inexperience may be found in older persons with whom analysis may languish because the environment falls in with the person's deficiencies.

*Summary*

At this point a summary of this discussion may be in order. Resistance as a term is perhaps best restricted to specifically willed opposition to insight or change, in or close to consciousness. The concept must involve the possibility of choice for in therapy we refer to it whenever we feel the issue of the moment may yield to an exercise of will. The less any therapeutic stalemate or difficulty can be affected by will or choice the less it can be ascribed to resistance. The expression of willed opposition, however, is an inadequate index of simple resistance, for as was suggested earlier, what is sometimes expressed as resistance is a matter of choice only in the sense that there is no other choice. Whether what one encounters is simple resistance or the broader condition I have called inertia depends not on what is expressed but rather on whether the problem can be influenced even temporarily by an act of will. Inertia seems a more useful term to describe the general condition of drag or fixity in relation to change because it more readily encompasses the deterministic aspects of personality as well as the volitional. The less the problem of general resistance is conceived of as a specific kind of negative motivation, the more it leads to the analysis of all sorts of conditions. Inertia is a function of a unique balance of characterological and existential factors, among which simple resistance is only one consideration. Ultimately it is this balance of forces that needs to be affected in psychotherapy if the person is to move off center. The analysis of simple resistance is one modest way of modifying this balance.

## Resistance and Therapy

As for therapeutic procedures in regard to resistance, the remarks that follow apply mostly to simple resistance rather than inertia, because work with the latter is more or less therapy in general.

Throughout therapy a certain balance is maintained between the forces that foster change and those that oppose it. This balance has to be continuously gauged to determine whether or not the person has room for maneuver. Though such determinations are sometimes difficult to make, when there is a requisite degree of freedom then the interpretation of simple resistance may be useful. The garden-variety type of resistance in therapy consists of a reluctance to see or act on certain things about oneself. In these instances the resistance, although not massive, is by no means insignificant. Simply bringing the reluctance to the person's attention frequently releases enough energy to overcome the temporary resistance. For example, a man who has been in therapy for about a year remarks at the beginning of an hour that somehow he has nothing to say. He elaborates on this theme for a time, although in the therapist's judgment he easily has the resources to overcome this kind of stalemate. The therapist then comments that it is hard to understand how he or any other person could go through a day let alone a week and not have a moment of doubt, unease, or difficulty. It could only mean that he has not been looking. Almost immediately there is a flow of experiences in relation to his sixteen-year-old son —certain childlike ways the boy retains, which the father usually tries not to notice and in fact never quite deals with. Apart from the characterological implications of this situation, the work draws close to a certain infantile strain, glimpsed only vaguely thus far, which runs through the entire family structure.

This type of approach is useful now and then even in dissolving the resistance that blocks associations to a particular dream symbol. When I encounter a person who says that at the moment he somehow has no associations whatever to a certain symbol, on occasion I may say: "This image must have a meaning to you because it is your image. You drew it out of your own experience precisely because it has a special meaning for you and would contribute to the larger experience of the dream. Perhaps it

is hard to reach at the moment but the image is not nonsense, the meaning is somewhere in you." More than once
such a comment has led to associations that clearly illuminated the dream symbol.

The degree of leverage afforded by the interpretation
of simple resistance is not sufficient, however, to sustain the
movement of therapy even over the length of a session.
Normally, the therapist needs to participate in such a way
that a momentum is gained which carries the work over
resistance whether or not a reference is made to it. Consider the example of a supervisory teacher in a private
school who begins a session by saying he will have to describe some of the events of his day to come to the point
he wishes to make. On this particular day he had planned
to hold one of a series of seminars with some trainees. But
because he was very busy, he met with them only briefly,
mainly to tell them that although he had material prepared
for the session, he would not be able to get into it because
he had to get back to his office. He hoped they would be
returning next semester so they could get the full training
he had planned for them. Those who would not be back
unfortunately would lose some of this, but it could not be
helped because there were a number of pressing things to
which he had to attend.

Though this is developed at some length, it is, he tells
the therapist, merely an introduction to what he wants to
get to. At this same meeting, he continues, two of the fe-
male trainees ask in which direction he is driving at the
end of the day, apparently hoping for a lift to the bus stop.
Jokingly he says to one of the trainees, "Why? Do you
want to come home with me?" To this the trainee replies,
"But you haven't asked me." This he says is the main

153

thing, for it set him ruminating that it looks as though people find him a good deal more attractive than he realized.

It should be mentioned that this teacher had previously cancelled a number of training sessions; somehow he never brought up these events in therapy, even though the therapist had the feeling that the teacher probably was not carrying his training responsibilities adequately. As he describes the day, he gives more detail about the seminar than the "main point" requires and yet little enough so that one could not know what the seminar and cancellation were really about. In offering this latter material he mumbles more than usual and brushes over certain aspects of it hurriedly; there is a definite note of self-justification in his explanation of the cancellation. Altogether this suggests the operation of resistance. Without touching upon the resistance, such an event can be opened up so that the realities emerge despite the resistance. What was the cancellation about? What other business was pressing upon him? Could he have attended to these developments at a later time? What was the session to be about? What specifically was he going to do in the course of the session? What had he prepared in relation to the seminar? What is this training program about? What is his place in the program? This is not to say that these questions are to be put to him in the form of an interrogation. Rather they define issues that have to be illuminated if the reality of the person's supervision is to come through. How one proceeds from one issue to the next is a function of what material develops and of the therapist's skill and grace.

The point here is that reality is an even more powerful counter to resistance than interpretation. It is less that the therapist discloses the truth to the person than that it is brought home to him by the encounter with the actualities of his life. The therapist contributes by knowing how to bring reality into the therapeutic experience and by helping to keep it steadily in focus. Material so developed tends to be less under the control of the defenses and of resistance. When reality has diminished force and intensity, as in the lives of people who are cloistered, routinized, or otherwise in retreat, there is little chance for psychotherapy. The young man dropped from college for academic failure is unlikely to solve his problems working as a clerk in the family business. Such arrangements permit resistance to prevail because reality is neither strong nor unrestrained enough to override it.

Although resistance is a difficult issue in every case, not infrequently therapy is attempted with people whose level of resistance is very high. The desire for change, an elementary necessity for this work, may be all but absent. The situation, however, is not simply negative, for what one meets is a subconscious insistence by the individual on remaining as he is. This is rarely an isolated condition, but it can remain in force despite sustained efforts to deal with factors that may be stifling the wish to move ahead.

Such a situation requires a maximum of patience and utter realism on the therapist's part. There is unlikely to be much movement, and on the occasions when this becomes apparent, it has to be brought out repeatedly with all the relentless reality available in the events. As long as the person is willing to face the failure and still somehow wants to go on, there is perhaps a basis for continuing to try, sometimes even for two or more years.

There may come a time under these rather extreme, but

not rare, conditions when it is better to stop than drag on. This alternative can be considered when the therapist feels that there has been a sustained trial in which everything has been done that he and the person know how to do. Frequently a person may not accept the therapist's view that not enough is happening, even though this has been demonstrated many times. In such instances words do not seem to get across. Through terminating therapy the person may be brought to realize for the first time that the therapist really believes that there are circumstances under which this work cannot be done (though some of these limits may well be the therapist's own). If the person ever initiates therapy again, he may know better the kind of call therapy makes upon him.

# Seven

## DREAM THOUGHT
## AND DREAMS

*REUD* demonstrated irrevocably that dreams, far from being nonsense, reveal significant aspects of personality. Yet he was not content to use the dream simply as a diagnostic tool. Every facet of the dream engaged him because he understood very well that dreams can throw light unexpectedly on general problems of psychology. Along this line he always regarded thought processes in dreams as an especially promising subject for study. This direc-

157

tion will be followed in this chapter in an effort to develop some of the implications for dream theory that may be derived from a direct examination of the structure of dream thought.

## The Dream As Analogy

Dream thought is defined by the most obvious feature of its structure—namely, that it is made up of images. At the moment of dreaming, dreams do not consist of words, ideas, concepts, or abstractions. When a person dreams he is fording a river; he simply sees and experiences himself doing so. If during the dream he slips and falls into the torrent, he finds himself "actually" gasping and struggling to hold on to some rocks. The inexorable series of images afford, as nocturnal cries and starts attest, the most literal sense of such activity.

Images, then, are the very stuff of which dreams are made. They may be thought of as living pictures that reconstruct or duplicate things or people known to us in life. In fact the word *image* is derived from the Latin verb *imitari,* which means *to imitate.* Many dreams contain images that are simply reproductions of actual objects or creatures. A person, for example, troubled about the way he uses his mind, might have a dream that consists of a realistic close-up of his head. From this we might gather that he is concerned about some aspect of his mental disposition, but we could not say much about his mind because the image hews too true to the fact.

Images may be reproductions of this kind or with the appearance of another dimension they became symbols. If our puzzled dreamer were to have a dream in which the top of his head takes on the vague outlines of a computer, we would have more than an image: we would have a symbol. We would also have an immediate sense of how he uses his head. An image thus becomes a symbol when it deviates from the actual object and contains a meaning that cannot be inferred from the literal image. In his use of this symbol the dreamer, in effect, draws a comparison between his own head and something that he senses is very much like it. Two images are juxtaposed in such a way that the difference between them provides a basis for defining more fundamental similarities.

Because dreams consist essentially of images and symbols, the main kinds of thinking in dreams are necessarily those of duplication and comparison. These processes are intrinsic to images and symbols. Other modes of thinking such as reasoning, analysis, and inference are not central in the dream structure.

The processes that predominate in the dream work are also at the heart of the analogical mode of thinking. In analogical thought we start with what is known (duplication, identification of the issue or question), then a comparison is drawn to something else in such a way as to extend our understanding of the known (symbolization). This suggests that the dream is nothing more or less than a highly individual analogy. The dreamer seems to be saying to himself, "This thing or event I'm concerned about—this is what it resembles."

The dream, however, is a very special kind of analogy. To begin with, it is formulated without direction or consciousness. For that matter it is not even experienced as thought, but rather as reality. These and other conditions affect the entire dream process and render the analogy that emerges unique in many respects.

Analogies in dreams are not built on processes of abstraction and reasoning but rather are developed in terms of concrete sensory and preceptual experiences. The dream is, in effect, an event, a situation in which something happens. The dreamer thus is thinking about things in a way not usually associated with thinking.

Perception in dreams has a sharpness and an immediacy that surely affects meanings. Dream experience is qualitatively similar to being on the scene, at the ringside, for example, where the thud of bone upon flesh is very different from what it seems like as it comes over television. The urgent reality of dreams gives impact to the meaning of whatever comparisons are being drawn. Even when a person is unable to formulate the meaning of a particular dream, often he is shaken by the experience.

Dream thought is essentially organismic in character. The basic unit of dream thought, the symbol, emerges from the senses as well as the intellect. Sensations, feelings, and perceptions in dreams give rise to new compounds of sensation, feeling, and perception. Symbols are the ultimate mental condensations of total experience. The symbol does not derive primarily from other thoughts, but rather from the whole person going through events and actualities.

The analogy in a dream, then, is fired under special conditions of realness, contact, and impact and during a time when the whole person is stirred and involved. These conditions give rise to the common experience that dream thought leaves one more with a sense of things then with an idea of them. Thought in dreams is very much like the thought evoked through seeing a play. No good play makes its point by means of logical discourse. In fact the main point rarely is stated in so many words. Rather, its effects are worked by drawing the onlooker into the experience so that he lives what the characters in the play are going through. With the onlooker thus involved the playwright can be confident that his point will get across in a way that counts.

## Analogical Thought

Little will be said here about the analogical mode of thought, although this subject warrants intensive study in its own right. Certain types of analogies have long been regarded as peculiarly effective means of reaching people. Among these are parables, allegories, poems, and plays, all of which hold up an analogy to some aspect of life and which in many respects are closely akin to dreams. Some types of parables have so much the quality of dream material that they can scarcely be distinguished from each other. Dreams, of course, do not consist of words, yet it is significant that parables like dreams, use a language rich in imagery.

In an article on methodology, Oppenheimer points out that many breakthroughs in the history of physics were made by men who approached new phenomena in straightforward analogical fashion.[1] The perception of likeness existing in difference appears to be an important mode of thought penetration. As far as understanding people is concerned, the analogy may be particularly useful because it

1. Robert Oppenheimer, "Analogy in Science," *American Psychologist*, XIII (1956), pp. 127–135.

is really a way of taking a fresh look at the familiar. The familiar is all too close to be easily understood. Comparisons apparently provide the leverage for getting beyond literalness.

In their inception dream analogies are highly individual expressions. They proceed from what the person knows, from the known to the known and yet curiously in the process something unknown gets defined. These analogies emerge from personal knowledge, filtered out of actual events. They are a close-to-data type of thinking, linked to problems not essentially by higher thought processes, but rather through an experiential sense of likeness. Dreams then, have a definable chemistry of thought, further study of which could well throw light on processes of effective learning and knowing.

## Implications

A persistent thread which runs through this discussion is that dreams are a particular form of thinking about one's general interests and concerns. Characteristically thought in dreams takes the form of sensory analogies. By its very nature an analogy is directed toward deepening comprehension. During waking life man's energy is taken up with what involves or troubles him. Such unresolved experiences as a challenging problem or an embarrassing event are likely to continue to fill his waking (though not necessarily conscious) thought and probably are further turned over in his mind under conditions of sleep.

This description of the natural action of thought in dreams stands in the stream of Jung's and Fromm's work, although it runs counter to certain of Freud's ideas. In contrast to Freud, both Fromm and Jung emphasize the questing, productive, adaptive qualities of the dream. The differences among these men on the function of dream thought is evident in their general theories on dreams.

According to Freud "dreams are given their shape . . . by the operation of two psychical forces [or systems]; . . . one of these forces constructs the wish which is expressed by the dream, while the other exercises a censorship upon the dream wish and . . . forcibly brings about a distortion in the expression of the wish."[2] Dreams are thus an illusory stage on which forbidden desires are fulfilled in disguised form. For Jung, however, "the dream describes the inner situation of the dreamer. . . . It shows the inner truth and reality of the patient as it really is."[3] Although one can take issue with Jung's map of inner reality, still he sees dreams as attempts to formulate problems and even solutions to these problems. As a result of this emphasis his approach has been characterized as prospective or forward-looking. For Fromm, ". . . dreaming is a meaningful and significant expression of any kind of mental activity under the conditions of sleep"[4] Mental activity during dreams, says Fromm, can include not only the expression of irrational strivings, but also acts of intelligence, judgment and even wisdom.

Even this brief review shows how fundamentally these

2. Sigmund Freud, *The Interpretation of Dreams* (New York: Basic Books, 1956), p. 144.

3. Carl Jung, *The Practice of Psychotherapy*, in *Collected Works*, XVI (New York: Pantheon Press, 1954), p. 142.

4. Erich Fromm, *The Forgotten Language* (New York: Rinehart, 1951), p. 25.

men diverge on the nature of thought in dreams. Freud, on the one hand, regards thought as the servant, even the plaything, of two contending systems. Thought merely provides imaginary forms through which one system—the id (instinctual wishes)—can furtively seek its satisfactions without too obviously offending the sensibilities of the second (the ego and superego). Should the compromise not work out satisfactorily, it may lead to the awakening of the sleeper. In this framework thought is a harried little faculty trying to placate everyone. For Fromm and Jung, however, dreams as a manifestation of thought, retain the significant functions associated with thought in waking life.

Despite the vagaries of thought, which no one has demonstrated better than Freud, it would be strange were thought in dreams to have none of the usefulness it has in everyday life. It is, after all, the range, penetration and productive character of man's thought which is his most fundamental power. Though its inefficiencies are conspicuous, thought still is commonly directed toward inquiry, comprehension and problem-solving. Little of the functional character of thought is retained in Freud's conception of the dream. In fact, for Freud, "secondary" functions such as ". . . thinking ahead, forming intentions, framing attempted solutions . . ." are given short shrift as having ". . . no claim to be considered part of the subject of dream interpretation."[5]

Freud's opinion that dreams always are generated by instinctual infantile wishes led to wide but unwarranted agreement that dreams are exclusively about personal problems. An artifact which effects the study of dreams has tended to support this impression. Most dreams are

5. Freud, *The Interpretation of Dreams*, p. 579.

obtained from people involved in psychotherapy, who naturally are concerned mainly with their own problems at the moment. As a consequence their dreams are almost invariably about their own personal characteristics. If one credits the functional nature of thought, however, there is every reason for dreams to deal with nonpersonal problems as well. Instances of such dreams are available in the literature, but these have been discounted by those who believe that every dream reveals some veiled aspect of oneself. (In some sense it does, of course. One can hardly buy a pound of flour without revealing some aspect of oneself.) Yet, in 1865, Friedrich Kekule come upon the concept of the benzene ring, a major discovery in organic chemistry, through a dream in which he saw atoms dancing in a ring.[6] (In those days people were still unselfconscious enough to dream about something besides themselves.) More to the point, however, is the example of complex, nonpersonal intellectual problems being solved through the medium of dream imagery.

Unless one is involved with idle distinctions, one's view of dreams should affect the way in which one understands and works with dreams. Because symbols give dreams their unique constitution, one's conception of symbols marks the way for the understanding of dreams. Implied in every conception for understanding dreams is a system for comprehending symbols.

The classic view of symbols in dreams is well respresented in Sharpe's statement that "the chief method of distorting the latent thoughts is accomplished by symbol-

6. Described in Alexander Findlay, *A Hundred Years of Chemistry* (London: Duckworth, 1948), pp. 36–38.

ism."[7] Forbidden wishes find expression under the disguise provided by symbols, Censorship seemed to Freud the most reasonable explanation for the failure of the dream to express its theme directly and logically. By the time Freud encountered the dream, he had long since been impressed with the extent of covert and suppressive operations in his patients. The obscure form of the dream could readily be understood as yet another instance of camouflage.

Disguise is effected, according to Freud, by the selection of images that differ from the actual object or thought. To take the image at face value would thus be misleading. Despite the gross difference, says Freud, the object and symbol have some quality in common, which becomes the basis for identifying the hidden thought. Usually this resemblance in terms of either form or feeling is so slight it can easily be overlooked by the conscious mind.

Freud's theory of symbols seems in several respects to take the secret code as a model. In this framework the symbol is designed to conceal real meaning; the aspects of the symbol that have nothing in common with the hidden idea constitute the disguise. Once the disguise is penetrated, once the hidden common element is discovered, then the symbol has no further value. This orientation colors Freud's theory, modified by his appreciation of the idiosyncratic rather than standard character of the symbol. The extent of distortion anticipated by those who take this view of symbols is evident in Healy's summary of the formidable list of disguises dreams may assume. "In . . . dream interpretation recognition is required of opposites, distortions, reversals, absurdities which are distortions welcomed

7. Ella Freeman Sharpe, *Dream Analysis* (London: Hogarth Press, 1951), p. 53.

by resistance, transpositions, twisting, modifications, trans-
formations, references, representatives, symbolizations,
fusions, combinations, allusions, hidden connections, and
motivations, contradictions, substitutions, displacements,
reminiscences, wishes—superficial as against deeper, ex-
pediences, conjurings up, inversions, repressions, elabora-
tions, interchanges." In tones of no little awe Healy then
notes the "immense skill" and "ingenuity" required to
interpret dreams.[8]

Many features of Freud's interpretive methods are consistent with this expectation. No dream, he says, can be
understood on the basis of its surface content. The dream
content per se is only a facade; buried in the images of
the "manifest content" lie the true or "latent thoughts,"
which can be reached only by a special approach.

Modern work with dreams rests largely on Freud's discovery of this approach, the method of free association to
all elements of the dream. This method greatly advanced
the study of dreams (however, not altogether for the reasons Freud assumed). No one can read Freud's associations to his dream about "Irma" without being impressed
with the inevitable intelligibility and coherence of dreams.[9]
Yet this dream can be understood in large measure on the
basis of the preamble (which tells about the events preceding the dream and thus gives the topic of the dream)
and the dream content itself. Furthermore, Freud does not
use symbols in a fashion entirely consistent with his theory.
In these associations he does not seem to be laboring to

8. William Healy, Augusta F. Bronner, and Anna Mae Bowers, *The
Structure and Meaning of Psychoanalysis* (New York: Alfred A.
Knopf, 1930), p. 277.
9. Freud, *The Interpretation of Dreams*, pp. 106–121.

penetrate a disguise; he does not strike up against unexpected twists, devices, tricks, blind alleys; he does not have to start over and over again. On the contrary, as often occurs in the searching, nonresistant person, there is in the associations a steadily expanding communication of meaning that immediately illuminates the symbols.

The entire venture had less the quality of breaking into a secret than entering almost by invitation into a person's private meanings. Rather than the decoding of cryptograms, the process is more like translating one known language into another, transposing poetry into prose, recasting portraits into the forms of concepts and everyday logic.

In his practical work with dreams Freud did far more with a symbol than establish its connection to a hidden thought. As is often the case with Freud, his work is larger than his theory, which sometimes leaves one feeling that a particular theoretical characterization does not quite do him justice. Nevertheless his theory had concrete effects upon his way of working, perhaps increasingly as the theory took him more and more in hand. Apart from those already mentioned, these effects are visible in a variety of ways. Explicit appreciation of the descriptive power of the symbol, for example, would never permit the equation of such images as poles, spires, rifles, and trees. Two men, one of whom visualizes his penis as a church spire, the other as a gun, undoubtedly would turn out to have rather different philosophies of sex. It is precisely the search for the "hidden" meaning of the symbol in dreams that leads to the neglect of the broader characterological implications of the symbol.

In the classical theoretical framework dream after

dream disappears with the identification of a standard libidinal striving or vaporous wish, none of which has hard and fast implications for personality (because it is only a wish, one doesn't really mean it). Freud's report of Sach's analysis of one of Bismarck's dreams provides a good example of what issues from this orientation.[10] In this dream Bismarck sees himself on a perilous path, saving Prussia from invading hordes with a wave of his riding crop, truly a Moses. This scene ultimately is resolved into a covert infantile wish on Bismarck's part to masturbate, though other implications are acknowledged to some extent. Such an interpretation is compatible with the conception of the dream as a safety-valve; whenever necessary a little excess steam is released. The assumption of particular hidden thoughts leads to emphasis on processes of identification rather than absorption, to the reduction rather than the expansion of meaning.

On first hearing, some dreams are so obscure that censorship springs to mind as a compelling explanation. Censorship exists mainly in the conscious person not in the thought product of his sleep. Distortion is assumed because of the apparent obscurity of the symbols. Does incomprehensibility, however, necessarily imply concealment? Symbols often are not easily understood because they grow out of individual experience and thus their meanings are frequently idiosyncratic. Upon awakening the person, resistant to knowing himself, need only influence the flow of available associations or meanings to render the symbols unintelligible. It is this combination of private meanings and waking personal resistance that produces the quality of obscurity. In cases of this sort the person may have little

10. Freud, *The Interpretation of Dreams,* pp. 378–381.

that comes to mind about the crucial symbols or he may let loose with a flood of associations, drowning meaning with mass. The dreams of such people are often "obscure." Yet it is remarkable how such an individual may, with a change of mood, effortlessly bring forth certain meanings that dispel the shadows.

The conscious person as the source of obscurity in dreams is illustrated in an incident that took place around the analysis of a dream offered by the industrial designer described in the previous chapter. During the course of therapy, this person, confined by his relationship to his mother, reported this dream: "I am on trial for murder. In a large room. Some girls are at the desk. I go around and hug them and they cuddle with me." After getting nowhere with his associations, the therapist commented that it seemed curious for him to be playing around with girls when he is on trial for his life. In reply he said that he knew the charge was a mistake; he had not committed any crime really. For want of something better the therapist said that even if it were a false charge, it still might be bothersome enough to interfere with his desire to play around. At this point he suddenly said that the dream had something to do with masturbation. When asked what brought masturbation to mind he said it occurred to him because these girls had no faces and yet something to do with sex was going on. With further questioning he remarked that it had to do with sex because these girls were strangers, because it did not have to do with somebody, somebody he knows, that is. At this juncture either the therapist asked him to retell the dream or he did so spontaneously. "I am in a big room like a traffic court. Desk next to desk. I go around hugging and snuggling with different girls. Then I find I am on trial for murder." As the dream was dreamt, it is all too revealing. Involvement with girls is a crime. If there is to be any at all, it has to be superficial (strangers). In actual life he has consistently lost interest in sex if the relationship extended over any appreciable period of time.

It is not in the dreaming, then, that the distortion occurs, but rather in the reworking that takes place after awakening. This incident is familiar, of course, as an instance of secondary elaboration. At the same time it suggests that the dream's obscurity is related not to concealment inherent in the symbol but rather to the temporary unavailability of meanings already existing in the dreamer's mind. Until the person is able to release the private knowledge that for him "faceless girls" are associated with masturbation, the symbol may give the illusion of concealment. For this person "faceless girls" is not a disguise but rather an image that in a positive sense means masturbation or sex.

The fact that dreams do not deal with our experience in straight-forward and factual fashion frequently is taken as another support for the theory of censorship. After spending an evening with his father, a person has a dream that he has had many times before about being an officer aboard a sinking naval vessel. While this is going on he feels no alarm, wanders aimlessly about the ship, never getting to his post. Finally he meets the commanding officer who glares at him and asks, "Where the hell have you been?" If there is nothing to hide, why does he not dream directly of his father and the difficulty he had in withstanding him during the evening? The "indirectness" of this dream may be judged by comparing the major themes of his life with the themes in the dream. Throughout his childhood this person bided his time, waiting for the strength to deal with a harsh, contemptuous, domineering father. As an adult, the son, who was a sword collector, would, while wearing a saber, often enter into heated arguments with his father. Though widely read and drawn to scholarly work, he was employed as a field worker in national marketing surveys. Every penny he made was saved to support a series of plunges in the stock market. The overriding aim that organized his life was to make a killing that would put him ahead of his father financially. Financial success had always been the father's measure of a man. Despite one loss after another, the patient continued to play the market, even with pitifully small sums. One resolution after another to return to study or to settle in one place to make a life for himself, evaporated whenever a chance appeared that he might realize his aim. These themes have clear equivalents in his repetitive dream. There is the picture of distant involvement with a superior, with overtones of contest and resistance. Apart from unconscious reaction to implicit direction, his behavior is aimless and self-destructive. All that goes on places him in great danger, although he has very little sense of this, which is very much the way it has been in actual life. Although the scene and actors may not be factual, can so direct a portrayal of his life, even though imaginative, be considered an instance of distortion?

Are such displaced images then the result of censorship, or are they products characteristic of a special mode of thinking? Silberer's work, at first appreciatively described by Freud,[11] suggested long ago that defensive factors may

11. Freud, *The Interpretation of Dreams*, pp. 344–345.

not be central in the shaping of images. Silberer attempted to observe during states of drowsiness or fatigue how thoughts may be transformed into images. On one occasion, in a condition of near sleep, he was turning over in his mind the need to revise an uneven passage in an essay. Suddenly the thought vanished and in its place he saw himself planing a piece of wood. Recently, I had, without intention, a similar experience and was struck by the instantaneous and total replacement of a thought by an image. One afternoon while resting and in a state of drowsiness approaching sleep, I had been thinking over a situation that I had handled badly. Abruptly my thoughts disappeared, supplanted by an image of me cutting my finger.

Silberer's image does not deal directly with the task of altering his essay. In the image per se this problem is nowhere to be seen. It is hard to see how censorship could be operating to produce so expressive an image. If anything images are created because they often convey so much more than literal or logical concepts. On the death of his mistress an ancient Chinese emperor wrote,

> The sound of her silk skirt has stopped.
> On the marble pavement dust grows.
> Her empty room is cold and still.
> Fallen leaves are piled against the doors. . . .[12]

No direct statement of his grief could ever have the meaning these images bring home to us. The poet limited to exposition instead of images loses much of his power to generate meaning, especially meaning evocative of feeling.

12. Arthur Waley, *Translations From the Chinese* (New York: Alfred A. Knopf, 1945), p. 49.

In any event, it has to be noted that the sensory language of the dream is relatively constant throughout life. It does not change with the lifting of repressions; even the best-analyzed person continues to dream in much the same way he always dreamed. Under conditions of sleep, thinking takes on unique forms, whether or not unacceptable issues are involved. Even Kekule's dream solution of the benzene ring problem, hardly a censorious subject, took the shape of displaced imagery. Comparisons require difference rather than identity, but difference does not necessarily disguise meaning.

The dream symbol does not so much stand *for* an object as it stands *beside* the object. It stands for itself; its meaning is the thought that emerges from the direct sensory experience of the symbol. At the same time it has an analogical relationship to the object. The symbol is less substitutive than it is complementary. The vital element is not the point of identity with the object, but rather what in its structure goes beyond this identity.

Once the topic of the dream is known (which is not difficult to determine), then the various symbols are often immediately infused with meaning. The symbols should be absorbed naively, wholly in their own terms, or else the meaning may be missed. Once aware in the mind-computer example that the person is concerned about his mind, then the main symbol has no element of distortion; the meaning is available in our sense of the precise, mechanical, repetitive, predetermined qualities of the computer. Associations are needed when the dream situation is undeveloped or when the symbols have a highly individual character; but there are many fully developed dreams that can be understood with few or no associations.

This point of view calls into question the concepts of censorship, distortion, and manifest vs. latent content, as well as the assumption that dreams cannot be interpreted without associations. It maintains that dreams need to be absorbed literally. One need not be wary that symbols "misrepresent" the issues. There is only one content, the symbols themselves; properly apprehended they yield the interpretation of the dream. The model of the secret code, the suspicion of distortion, makes for distance and brings into play faculties of ingenuity, reasoning, cleverness, artfulness, which, I believe, interferes with the understanding of dreams.

Nothing so discourages clinicians as to sit with a group of colleagues and hear as many interpretations of a dream as there are interpreters present. This results from the failure to approach the dream in terms of its unique language. Fewer meanings arise from direct experience as compared to the number available through cogitation. The latter need only satisfy considerations of logic as opposed to considerations of actuality. Our naval officer dreams he is on a ship that is going down, but he feels no alarm. If one reasons about this in relation to various assumptions about dreams, many possibilities seem plausible. Perhaps he has the sense of sinking without fright into the depths of his unconscious (the ocean); perhaps this is a return to the watery womb; perhaps because he feels no fear but is sinking into the all-embracing, surging sea, it is a veiled sexual experience with the mother; and so on ad infinitum. Yet if one responds unfettered by assumptions and places oneself in the position of literally going through this experience, the possible meanings are few indeed. Would not one aspect of it have to be something like, "I am in

175

great danger and don't even feel it." Such difficulty as we may have in understanding dreams relates mostly to our being unaccustomed to responding in terms of the special language of dreams.

The attempt to teach someone to understand this language is a little like trying to tell a person how to find jokes funny. People can do this very well providing they do not think too much while doing it. We are less in need of instruction about it than we are in need of practice in reacting in a particular mode. What goes into dream interpretation is not so much technique or intellectual manipulation as the use of certain primary abilities. Being able to let oneself into an experience is perhaps the fundamental process involved, but this is easier said than done.

# AIMS AND OUTCOMES
# IN PSYCHOTHERAPY

*T IS* a commentary of sorts that at the very last, after having described psychotherapy at length, we take up the question of what we are trying to do in this work. One would think that a respectable scientific field ought to be able to set down its objectives at the outset and then indicate how these aims are to be implemented. Still, the sequence in this book corresponds to the historical record, for psychologists have discovered more or less what they are trying to do mostly in the process of doing it.

*Difficulties in Defining Goals*

Psychotherapy has aimed, of course, at the amelioration of psychological difficulties, but this general objective has had different meanings at different times. In the history of psychotherapy the meaning of amelioration has ranged from relief of symptoms to acceptable social adjustment, from happiness or well-being to self-realization. Such ultimate aims, however, are themselves made up of congeries of secondary aims, including such diverse considerations as the recovery of early memories, the genital orgasm, "where there is id, there shall ego be," genuineness, self-insight, actualization of feeling, self-respect, productiveness, and so on. This random listing suggests that a neat system for the classification of therapeutic aims would be hard to design. Certain aims refer to personality traits (genuineness), some more to therapeutic methods (insight), and some to the combination of both (self-awareness). Some may be classified as more or less ultimate goals (productiveness), some as intermediate ones (recovery of early memories), and again some appear to be a combination of both (actualization of feeling).

Defining the aims of psychotherapy has thus been a perplexing and somewhat disorderly project, complicated in particular by the difficulty of separating means from ends in human psychology. Some aims have reference to means (self-awareness), some to ends (self-respect), and some to factors that seem to be both means and ends (actualization of feeling or self-awareness). The means–end dilemma and other difficulties in establishing aims derive from several characteristics of our subject matter. Among these, the interrelatedness of psychological systems and qualities,

the uniqueness of the person, and the emergent, evolution-
ary character of personality make, in combination, for a
goodly share of the difficulty encountered in the area of
aims. For example, the concept of evolution, in taking
cognizance of the stages of life, suggests that aims need to
be related to time of life. Jung writes, "the basic facts of
the psyche undergo a marked alteration in the course of
life; . . . we could almost speak of a psychology of life's
morning and [of its] afternoon."[1] For the younger person,
he believes, neurosis stems mainly from shrinking from
the necessity for expansion and from facing the world.
Older people, he suggests, may develop difficulties because
they cling to an attitude appropriate to youth, are unable
to accept "a contraction of forces," and fail to become involved in "the affirmation of what has been achieved."[2]
Moreover, if emergence is continuous throughout life, the
concept implies that we cannot know what forms and
reaches of human attributes may evolve in a particular
person in the course of a particular life experience. In
this sense our definitions of aims can never perhaps be
quite complete.

## Theories Concerning the Goals of Psychotherapy

A review of the thinking of major theorists may help in
seeing how the field has dealt with these difficulties and
also in attempting to develop a current position on the
problem. Historically formulations about aims appear to
have taken two directions. One has to do with a category

1. Jung, *Practice of Psychotherapy*, p. 39.
2. *Ibid.*

of which self-awareness is the foremost representative; the other deals with defining desirable end-traits of personality.

Freud defines the aim of psychotherapy in terms of the first category. The essential task of analysis, he writes, "consists in making the unconscious accessible to consciousness."[3] In this objective he is very thoroughgoing for he does not regard an analysis as complete until "all gaps in memory have been filled in, all the enigmatic products of mental life elucidated."[4] Carrying forward this objective Fenichel much later writes that psychoanalysis aims for the "full annulment of the repression."[5] Sullivan not only affirms this goal, but, if anything, gives it more weight. "The principal problem of the therapeutic interview is that of facilitating the accession to awareness of information which will clarify for the patient the more troublesome aspects of his life."[6] Lack of awareness, he feels, is the essential answer to be offered to the person who asks, "What ails me? How can I get better? Why can't I overcome this habit?"[7] Indeed, as he puts it, "one achieves mental health to the extent that one becomes aware of one's interpersonal relations."[8] Self-awareness thus becomes for Sullivan the criterion of mental health.[9]

3. Freud, *Collected Papers*, I, p. 269.
4. *Ibid.*, p. 269.
5. Fenichel, p. 556.
6. Harry Stack Sullivan, "Conceptions of Modern Psychiatry," *Psychiatry*, III (1940), p. 91.
7. *Ibid.*, p. 102.
8. *Ibid.*
9. There are very real limits to such a criterion of mental health. It is entirely possible, for example, for a person to know that he is ruthless or tricky and even take a certain pride in it. Whether such

Yet neither Freud nor Sullivan regard self-awareness as the final end of development. Speaking for orthodox psychoanalysis, Fenichel holds that "the undoing of the repression enables the infantile sexual strivings to participate in the development of the personality,"[10] which suggests the expectation of further growth. For Sullivan, with the development of self-awareness, there follows an unfolding of the self "to such final effect that the patient as known to himself is much the same person as the patient behaving with others. This is 'psychiatric' cure."[11] Although expansion is anticipated by Sullivan, the expansion is defined, at least in part, in terms of the accuracy of self-knowledge. Both viewpoints, however, concur on the assumption that awareness leads to further expansion of the self.

The efforts to define this further development of personality set the second direction taken in the formulation of aims, that of describing end-traits of personality that should be realized through psychotherapy. Fenichel, for example, believes that the satisfactory release of libidinal energy "makes for the full development of love (and hate) [and] means the end of reaction formations and an increase in the ability to sublimate anymore. . . ." Emotions then are not warded off anymore. . . ."[12] In this conception of the genital (normal) character are a number of qualities

a person would be regarded as a model of mental health is doubtful. This criterion furthermore stands in some contradiction to Sullivan's own view that with self-awareness there follows a further and necessary expansion of the personality. In short, he himself suggests, without explicitly resolving the contradiction, that self-awareness may not be a sufficient criterion of health and development.

10. Fenichel, p. 556.
11. Sullivan, "Conceptions of Modern Psychiatry," p. 117.
12. Fenichel, p. 496.

associated with the mature person: sexual adequacy, capacity for strong and significant feelings, genuineness (end of reaction formation), and broadening of interests (sublimation). For Sullivan, the mature person is characterized by adequate self-respect, respect for others, a capacity for intimacy, and the dignity and personal initiative adequate to one's station in life.[13] In this description we have again a list of qualities to which few therapists would take exception. For Fromm, the developed person may be described as productive, that is, able "to use his powers and to realize the potentialities inherent in him. If we say he must use his powers we imply he must be free and not dependent. . . . We imply, furthermore, that he is guided by reason, since he can make use of his powers only if he knows what they are. Productiveness means that he experiences himself as the embodiment of his powers."[14] Among these powers Fromm lists reason, imagination, and love. In Fromm's view, then, the fully mature person is capable of using his own powers and is free, independent, and loving.

## Sifting These Views For Directions

As can be seen, these descriptions overlap somewhat and, although not identical, can hardly be said to contradict one another. Indeed there seems to be a certain consensus among therapists about desirable end-traits. Curiously, however, therapists have been reluctant simply to

13. Sullivan, "Conceptions of Modern Psychiatry," p. 28.
14. Erich Fromm, *Man For Himself* (New York: Holt, Rinehart and Winston, 1947), p. 84.

define such traits and then set them down as the aims of psychotherapy. For a long time it ran counter to the image of the scientist to be involved in any way with issues of valuation and desirability. The belated acknowledgment that clinicians are constantly judging personality development in terms of the broad values of civilization (and increasingly in terms of a slowly accumulating body of empirical information on psychological growth) eased one of the restrictions blocking study of this general area. Therapists, furthermore, were reluctant to set goals that they had no sure methods of achieving. Under these circumstances emphasis on such goals would leave them preaching rather than helping. Then, too, should therapists aim for all the positive traits, and if not all, which ones, and why these? Aiming for all is obviously unrealistic and selecting among desirable possibilities, dignity versus vivacity, for example, is nonsensical. Furthermore, because people are not likely to achieve an end in the same way, precise definitions of such ends are restrictive and difficult to work out. A humorless independence of mind is not quite the same as independence tempered by generosity. There are reasons enough then for therapists not to have followed the disarmingly easy course of listing and aiming for desirable end-traits.

Several questions arise from this brief survey. How is it that Freud, Sullivan, and others so persistently advanced self-insight as the cardinal aim of psychotherapy? Apart from the well-known grounds for its utility are there other bases for this emphasis? What comparisons may be drawn among the several formulations of aims and what are the implications of these comparisons?

Although most of the various characterizations of the

developed person seem to be more alike than different, concerning self-insight there is a noteworthy difference. Fromm does not minimize the utility of self-awareness, but he does not set it down as an explicit and central aim of psychotherapy. In his description of the developed person there is a mixture of specifications—end-traits on the one hand (freedom, independence) and the use of one's powers (reason, imagination) on the other. The latter especially strikes a fresh note in regard to aims and perhaps accounts for the variance we have come upon in relation to self-awareness.

Fromm does not specify self-awareness as an independent aim probably because it falls into a larger rubric he has in mind. Freud and Sullivan very likely emphasize self-awareness for the very reason that Fromm does not. They not only had a full appreciation of the clinical value of self-awareness but probably also sensed that it represented a category of important psychological processes. They knew very well that, clinically, self-awareness is a powerful antidote to chaos and disorganization—that is, to psychopathology. The way in which panic states yield to contact with the factors producing anxiety provides an impressive example of the effects of self-awareness. One of the most fearsome of human experiences is to feel acted upon by interior forces outside of one's knowledge or control, which is what occurs in pronounced states of dissociation. Yet this condition is produced by nothing more than lack of contact with self and these forces. Self-awareness engenders an experience of meaning and coherence. It helps to place one in the center of one's life; one feels one is living, not being lived. Indeed it may be said, to rephrase Sullivan, that a person in touch with himself has mental health to the degree that he is unlikely to develop severe symptomatology.

Self-awareness then contributes significantly to enabling the person to feel whole—that is, to a state of integration. Observation of this effect convinced Freud and Sullivan that they were dealing with an important factor in human functioning. Although they may well have appreciated that other factors also have a bearing on intactness, so far as I know none are explicitly defined or stressed in the fashion of self-awareness. As a result, they may have given to self-awareness the weight that belongs to the entire category.

The category to which self-awareness belongs represents the first of the two directions taken in defining the aims of psychotherapy. It may be designated by the term *integration,* which refers to the coordinate functioning of all the basic psychological factors, systems, and capacities of the human being. The adequate play of these systems produces at the minimum, a condition of intact functioning. Among the systems, factors, and powers that belong to this category, in addition to self-awareness, are: openness, sensitivity, capacity to feel, intensity, control, intelligence, reason, judgment, adequacy of contact, degree of use of own reactions, and need satisfactions. In contrast the second direction has been concerned with end-traits, examples of which are generosity, dignity, judiciousness, humaneness, and lovingness.

In elaborating the distinction between integration and end-traits, some clarification of the problem of defining aims may emerge. Integration, as has been suggested, refers to basic processes and capacities, end-traits to the results of development. Desirable end-traits are in effect potentials. They cannot be aimed for directly, they cannot be "put on." Rather end-traits come of their own, as by-products of a particular interaction between the relatively intact person and life experience. One can strive to feel more or to become more competent and then perhaps such functioning may be consummated in lovingness or dignity. In contrast it is unlikely that a direct effort to behave with dignity will result in competence. The higher reaches of development may be compared to the growth of a flowering plant. Without adequate photosynthesis, without an effectively functioning biologic process for synthesizing carbohydrates, the plant may never develop its flower. It may live and even achieve its essential shape, but still never realize its crowning potentials.

On this basis, it is doubtful that the achievement of desirable end-traits can be the direct and major aim of psychotherapy. It is even questionable that such traits can be defined precisely and still encompass unique variations of the traits. Yet some knowledge of desirable end-traits is of value for it enables people to perceive that there are alternatives to remoteness, righteousness, ignorance, inferiority, egocentricity, or arrogance, and even possibilities for human nature they may never have envisioned. As Gardner Murphy sees it, new choices become possible as knowledge extends our conception of what is attainable.[15] To have impact such knowledge has to be communicated in a special way, more by living it than by lecturing about it—but this is a problem in itself. There are limits, however, to how much one person can show another about the possibilities of life. Jung makes this point rather drastically: "We are in reality unable to borrow or absorb anything

15. Gardner Murphy, *Human Potentialities* (New York: Basic Books, 1958), pp. 3–14.

from the outside, from the world or from history. What is essential to us can grow only out of ourselves."[16] Knowledge of possibilities is indeed a far step from realization, but still possibilities can engender hope and respect and in this manner support the lengthy exploration required for achievement.

In my view this leaves integration, the category hinted at by the emphasis on self-awareness and explicitly indicated in Fromm's stress on "powers," as the immediate and essential goal of psychotherapy. Psychotherapy needs mainly to be concerned with bringing into play all of the basic processes and capacities in human functioning. A relatively intact person, using himself fully, who is interested in and has glimpsed the possibilities of life and development, is in my opinion very much on his way. I would be satisfied to achieve such a result in therapy. Such a person may and usually does have a long way to go in his "flowering." But this end need not be the specific concern of psychotherapy. Therapy cannot go on and on, nor need it go on into following the ultimate developmental reaches of a particular person. If the person is all there, then I would feel we have a good basis for expecting that significant traits and characteristics will emerge with time and experience.

16. Carl Jung, *The Integration of Personality* (New York: Farrar and Rinehart, 1939), p. 31.

# INDEX